Towards the Abyss

Volodymyr Ishchenko was born in Hoshcha in western Ukraine in 1982 to parents who worked on cybernetics and cosmonautics in Kiev. He taught sociology at Kiev universities and was active in the Ukrainian new left. He is now a researcher at the Freie Universität in Berlin. His writing has been published by the *Guardian*, *Al Jazeera*, *Jacobin* and *New Left Review*.

Towards the Abyss

Ukraine from Maidan to War

Volodymyr Ishchenko

VERSO

London • New York

First published by Verso 2024
© Volodymyr Ishchenko 2024

1 3 5 7 9 10 8 6 4 2

Verso
UK: 6 Meard Street, London W1F 0EG
US: 388 Atlantic Avenue, Brooklyn, NY 11217
versobooks.com

Verso is the imprint of New Left Books

ISBN-13: 978-1-80429-554-0
ISBN-13: 978-1-80429-556-4 (US EBK)
ISBN-13: 978-1-80429-555-7 (UK EBK)

British Library Cataloguing in Publication Data
A catalogue record for this book is available from the British Library

Library of Congress Cataloging-in-Publication Data

Names: Ishchenko, Volodymyr, author.
Title: Towards the abyss : Ukraine from Maidan to war / Volodymyr
  Ishchenko.
Other titles: Ukraine from Maidan to war
Description: London ; New York : Verso, 2024. | Includes bibliographical
  references.
Identifiers: LCCN 2023046448 (print) | LCCN 2023046449 (ebook) | ISBN
  9781804295540 (paperback) | ISBN 9781804295564 (ebook ; US) | ISBN
  9781804295557 (ebook ; UK)
Subjects: LCSH: Ukraine Conflict, 2014- | Russo-Ukrainian War, 2014- |
  Ukraine--Politics and government--2014- | Ukraine--Relations--Russia
  (Federation) | Russia (Federation)--Relations--Ukraine.
Classification: LCC DK5417 .I834 2024 (print) | LCC DK5417 (ebook) | DDC
  947.7086--dc23/eng/20231130
LC record available at https://lccn.loc.gov/2023046448
LC ebook record available at https://lccn.loc.gov/2023046449

Typeset in Fournier MT by Hewer Text UK Ltd, Edinburgh
Printed and bound by CPI Group (UK) Ltd, Croydon CR0 4YY

FSC
www.fsc.org
MIX
Paper | Supporting
responsible forestry
FSC® C171272

To my mother and father

Contents

Doomed, doomed and wretched. Or rather — happy and doomed, since they don't know they're doomed, that the mighty of their world see in them only a dirty tribe of ravishers . . . that for them everything is preordained and — worst of all — that historical truth here . . . is not on their side, they are relics, condemned to destruction by objective laws, and to assist them means to go against progress, to delay progress on some tiny sector of the front. Only that doesn't interest me . . . What has their progress to do with me, it's not my progress and I call it progress only because there's no other suitable word.

— Arkady and Boris Strugatsky, *The Snail on the Slope*

Acknowledgements

This book would not have been possible without the tremendous work of Tom Hazeldine of Verso Books, who went through all my opinion pieces, essays, and interviews over the course of nearly a decade, organizing and editing the selected texts. During this long period, I worked in various institutions in Ukraine and Germany. My political and polemical texts were not directly related to the teaching activities and projects I was working on. However, without the support of Svitlana Oksamytna, Pavlo Kutuev, Nina Potarska, Heiko Pleines, Gal Kirn, Christian Prunitsch, Mihai Varga, and Katharina Bluhm, it is not certain that I would have found time for them.

It should be clear from my references and mentions who have been important intellectual influences on me. However, Don Kalb, Georgi Derluguian, Lucan Ahmad Way, Dominique Arel, and Jesse Driscoll not only shaped my thinking about class and nation, the Soviet and post-Soviet period, Ukrainian politics and the war, but also provided human support as senior colleagues, even when they clearly disagreed with my views.

The analysis of the post-Soviet maidan revolutions and the crisis of hegemony would not have been possible without our long-standing collaboration with Oleg Zhuravlev, who read and provided important comments on early drafts of many of the texts in this collection. Our research with Oleksii Viedrov, Andrii Gladun, and Mykhailo Slukvin informed some of the conclusions about Euromaidan. I am also grateful to Yuri Dergunov for his advice, which helped to improve some of the essays. I am very glad that we were and remain comrades, despite the front that divided our country. Some of the texts also benefited greatly from discussions in the collective of *LeftEast* – an outlet of the Eastern European left. Of course, the views expressed in the texts and any mistakes are mine alone.

No words can express how grateful I am for my wife Tanyi's unlimited patience and understanding when some of these texts were taking me away from my family for too much time.

The chapters in this book draw on the following publications: Chapter 1: *Guardian*: 'Ukraine protests are no longer just about Europe', 22 January 2014; 'Ukraine has not experienced a genuine revolution, merely a change of elites', 28 February 2014, 'Maidan or anti-Maidan? The Ukraine situation requires more nuance', 15 April 2014; 'Ukraine has ignored the far right for too long – it must wake up to the danger', 13 November 2014; 'Ukraine's government bears more responsibility for ongoing conflict than the far-right', 4 September 2015; 'Kiev has a nasty case of anti-communist hysteria', 18 December 2015. Chapter 2: 'Maidan mythologies', *New Left Review* 93, May–June 2015. Chapter 3: 'A comedian in a drama', *Jacobin*, 24 April 2019. Chapter 4: 'From Ukraine with comparisons: Emerging notes on Belarus', *LeftEast*, 21 August 2020. Chapter 5: 'How *maidan* revolutions reproduce and intensify the post-Soviet crisis of political representation' (with Oleg Zhuravlev), PONARS Eurasia policy memo no. 714, 18 October 2021; 'Ukraine in the vicious circle of post-Soviet crisis of hegemony', *LeftEast*, 29 October 2021. Chapter 6: 'Three scenarios for the Ukraine-Russia crisis', *Al Jazeera*, 16 February 2022; 'Russia's war in Ukraine may finally end the post-Soviet condition', *The Parliament Magazine*, 21 March 2022; 'Why did Ukraine suspend 11 "pro-Russia" parties?', *Al Jazeera*, 21 March 2022; 'Russia's military Keynesianism', *Al Jazeera*, 26 October 2022. Chapter 7: 'NATO through Ukrainian eyes', in Grey Anderson, ed.,

Natopolitanism: The Atlantic Alliance since the Cold War, Verso, London and New York 2023. Chapter 8: 'Behind Russia's war is thirty years of post-Soviet class conflict', *Jacobin*, 3 October 2022. Chapter 9: 'Ukrainian voices?', *New Left Review* 138, Nov–Dec 2022. Interview: 'Towards the Abyss', *New Left Review* 133/134, Jan–Apr 2022.

Preface
A Wrong Ukrainian

There are several ways in which this book should *not* be read. You should not read it looking for some objective Truth about the war in Ukraine. You should not read me as a sympathetic 'Ukrainian voice' with whom you can repent your 'Western privilege'. I also hope you will not see the book in precisely the opposite way: as an attempt to 'sell' you a superficially sympathetic position that pushes the right buttons for an international audience but, if anything, serves the interests of reactionary political forces.

Sometimes my writing has indeed been read in these regrettable ways. As a social scientist, I try to advance a deeper understanding of protests, revolutions, far rights and radical lefts, civil societies, nationalisms and imperialisms, and I have been doing so for twenty years. Compared with my scholarly publishing, the chapters in this book are openly political and indeed polemical. They are passionate, which is not necessarily a bad thing, but not exactly an 'objective' yardstick by which to judge the war in Ukraine. Some of my conclusions sound strikingly prophetic today. Some have been proven wrong. For some, the jury is still out.*

---

* My thinking has been evolving since 2014, both as a result of escalating events and deeper engagement with them as a researcher. For this collection, I added a few retrospective endnotes to update the facts or analysis of the original texts when I felt it was necessary. These are indicated by square brackets in the notes section.

I am Ukrainian and lived in Kiev for most of my life, studying and teaching at Ukrainian universities and conducting research and media projects with Ukrainian NGOs. However, as you will read, I am highly sceptical of attempts to use national identity to claim the moral high ground. In Kiev I was active in small 'new left' initiatives from the early 2000s until I had to leave Ukraine in 2019. But none of the chapters in this book was written as a partisan of any political outfit.

How do I want this book to be read? My answer may sound surprising and perhaps like wishful thinking. I would like the book, with its rolling analysis of the beginning of the armed conflict in Ukraine, to be read first and foremost because it records reactions to *globally relevant* processes. Wherever you look, social and environmental problems are overlapping and reinforcing each other, creating what Adam Tooze terms a 'polycrisis'.[1] We have become accustomed to the feeling that next year will be worse than the last. Some people got this feeling with the pandemic in 2020, some with Brexit and the election of Donald Trump in 2015–16, some with the global economic crisis in 2008, some with 9/11 and the US wars in Afghanistan and Iraq. For most Ukrainians, the problems did not start with the 2022 invasion, or with the Euromaidan revolution and the war in Donbass in 2014. The feeling that the country was in a deep crisis, that it was developing in the wrong direction, that nobody in the political elite or state institutions could be trusted, has been spreading for decades, and at least since the 1990s, when systematic data on public opinion has become regularly available. Fresh hopes were raised by the *maidan*[*] revolutions of 2004 and 2014

---

* Ukraine's 'Orange Revolution' (2004) and 'Euromaidan' or 'Revolution of Dignity' (2014) both started at the central 'Maidan' square in Kiev, as had the earlier 'Revolution on Granite' (1990), and the word *maidan* is nowadays often applied to any massive anti-government street protests not only in Ukraine but in other post-Soviet countries as well. In this book, 'Euromaidan' and 'Maidan' refer interchangeably to the revolution of 2014, while the phrase '*maidan* revolutions' is used as a generic term for a type of loosely organized revolution with vaguely articulated claims and weak leadership; this is theorized in Chapter 5.

(see Chapter 5), by the election of Volodymyr Zelenskyi, a 'new face', in 2019 (Chapter 3) and by the spectacular failure of Russia's initial invasion plan and the Ukrainian victories in the first year of the full-scale war. But overall, the gloom has proved difficult to dispel.

One specific group has experienced this crisis particularly severely, to the point of its own disintegration as a political community – which at any rate provides a certain epistemological vantage point. Let's call this group Soviet Ukrainians, as distinct from Russian-speaking Ukrainians or those living in the southeastern regions of Ukraine. Rather than essentializing ethnolinguistic differences or regional political cultures, to understand Ukrainian political cleavages we should think about the dynamics of class and social revolution. *Towards the Abyss* grew out of the political activism and evolving intellectual reflection of a person who belongs 'organically' to this Soviet Ukrainian group. Since the beginning of the Euromaidan revolution in late 2013, I had had a growing feeling that things were getting worse and worse. There were disturbing signs that my country was sliding in a direction that held no promise, at least not for people like me. Until the very last moment, I remained hopeful about the prospects for a pluralistic Ukraine, as you can see from the opening passage of Chapter 6, written on the eve of the Russian invasion. But one of my first thoughts when I read the news in the early morning of 24 February 2022 was that no matter how this war ends, I will no longer have a homeland. I feel the same today.

For the predominantly peasant and illiterate population of the territory of present-day Ukraine in the 1920s, the processes of nation-building and social revolution were inextricably linked. Ukrainians were becoming a modern nation as part of an egalitarian revolutionary movement with universal appeal. Originally, the Bolsheviks were a party of an urban revolutionary intelligentsia that appealed to the working class. They had a problem winning majority support in the largely agrarian Russian Empire. In Ukraine, there were additional peculiarities. The Bolsheviks were an urban party in predominantly Russian, Jewish and Polish cities surrounded by Ukrainian-speaking peasants. There is a long tradition of analysing this problem through the prism of the 'Ukrainian national question'.[2] The weakness of this approach is its primordial and teleological conception of the Ukrainian nation. It assumes that Ukrainian peasants were somehow *presupposed* to adopt a specific variant of national identity propagated by the petty-bourgeois intelligentsia, when they were really more interested in land redistribution – a subject on which bourgeois nationalists took a fairly moderate position, not least because they needed the support of the imperialist powers: first Germany, then the Entente. The Bolsheviks succeeded in Ukraine less because of their views on the 'Ukrainian national question' than because they were the most revolutionary force in the Civil War.

The Bolsheviks came to power in what Gramsci famously called the 'war of manoeuvre', without securing a strong counter-hegemony over the majority; it was just that the competing forces were even weaker. This put the question of building a durable hegemony post-factum on the agenda of the new revolutionary state. Nationalism has been a typical means of constructing hegemony in modern states, allowing the interests of a particular class or class fraction to be presented as the interests of the whole nation. Therefore, it is not surprising that the new Soviet state turned to nation-building. There was genuine interest among the Bolsheviks in the liberation of oppressed nations, and lively debate about the various 'national questions' posed by the decline of the Romanov, Habsburg and Hohenzollern empires. In the 1920s, 'organic' cadres from the national minorities of the former Russian Empire were recruited en masse into nascent Soviet institutions. To overcome the illiteracy of the peasant majority, the Bolsheviks introduced mass schooling and promoted cultural development in national-minority languages. They also established quasi-independent nation-state structures within the Soviet Union, including the Ukrainian Soviet Socialist Republic.

But the Soviet approach to nationalism shifted in accordance with broader strategic imperatives. By the 1930s, with deteriorating prospects for the worldwide proletarian revolution and the consolidation of state socialism in one country, the usefulness of the above became doubtful. The 'affirmative action' policies were curtailed and national intelligentsias repressed, followed by wartime mobilization of Russian patriotism and creeping post-war Russification. The Soviet Union did not lead a world revolution, but it built a modern nation-state in the vast space vacated by the Russian Empire. At its heart was the idea of a civic nation of the 'Soviet people'. This imagined community unified all the diverse ethnicities of the Union within a socialist economy and culture, defined politically by loyalty to the communist project. In practice, as with any other civic nationalism, it was never ethnically 'neutral'. Russian culture underlay it, and the Russian language was the vernacular of social progress and individual career advancement. In these circumstances, the Ukrainian villagers who migrated to the cities after 1945 would start speaking Russian, including to their children. As Ukrainian and Russian are not that different anyway, this was typically perceived not so much in ethnic terms but rather as a switch from a 'rural' language to an 'urban' one.

Thus, by the time the Soviet Union collapsed, a large group of Russian-speaking Ukrainians had emerged in Ukraine (along with a fairly large group of ethnic Russians). They identified as Ukrainian – this was actually inscribed by the Soviet practice of including ethnonational identity in passports – but almost exclusively used the Russian language at home, with their family and friends, and, if not otherwise required, in education, at work and in interactions with the state.

Let me add some brief family history here. The westernmost part of Ukraine – Galicia – was united with the rest of the country during World War II. This is where my father was born – in Lviv, the largest city in the western regions. My mother was born in Hoshcha, a very small town in the Rivne region, which had also been part of Poland in the interwar period.

However, none of my grandparents were natives of these places. Ukraine took its present form under the Soviet Union, a society that facilitated a lot of horizontal mobility, without which my family could not have existed. Among my grandparents and great-grandparents, there were Ukrainians from both eastern and relatively western parts of the country, as well as Russians from the Moscow area, Poles and Belarusians. The grandfather whose surname I inherited came from Donbass – not the Russian-speaking, urban, working-class Donbass, but the rural and at that time predominantly Ukrainian-speaking Donbass north of the Lugansk region, which is now annexed by Russia. After World War II he moved to Lviv to study, where he met my Russian grandmother. They started a Russian-speaking family in Lviv, which was rapidly Ukrainianizing after losing its pre-war Polish and Jewish majority and becoming stereotyped as a sort of capital of 'Banderovite' nationalism.

What was even more impressive was the rapid vertical mobility that the Bolshevik Revolution had unleashed. The Lviv side of my family descended from a low-level clerk on a collective farm and a party commissar in the Red Army from a working-class family who rose to the military rank of major. My other two great-grandparents were a sugar-refinery worker and staunch Bolshevik activist, and a forest engineer. My grandparents were the first generation to finish a real higher education and to teach in schools and universities. My father, from Lviv, graduated from the prestigious Moscow Institute of Physics and Technology – commonly hailed as the 'Soviet MIT' – and worked on modelling the movements of Soviet spaceships at the Institute of Cybernetics in Kiev, which was founded and headed by Viktor Glushkov, the creator of the first personal computer in the Soviet Union and particularly famous for the National Automated System for Computation and Information Processing. Some believe that this unrealized project for the 'Soviet Internet' could have solved some of the biggest problems of the centralized planned economy. My father and mother met at Glushkov's Institute and started a Russian-speaking family in Kiev.

The grandmother who helped raise me was a teacher of Russian language and literature, although she came from a Ukrainian village. The works of classical Russian poets, whose names and monuments are now erased from Ukrainian streets, were the first books she read to me and the first poems I could recite by heart. Was this 'colonization'? Did the Ukrainian speakers in my family feel oppressed when they spoke in Russian? On the contrary, it was the language of their loving partners, of the big cities, of higher education, the language spoken by most of their peers and colleagues in the technical intelligentsia. For them, it was not the language of oppression, but of advancement. As for the millions of other Soviet Ukrainian families.

Our 'Russification' was part of a modernizing transformation of revolutionary magnitude. I can tell my son that one of his grandfathers worked with spaceships, and another grandfather worked with blueprints of *Mriia* (meaning 'Dream' in Ukrainian) – the largest airplane on Earth, built in the late 1980s by the Antonov aircraft plant in Kiev to transport some of those spaceships. How many of my son's generation will be able to tell their children something similar? *Mriia* was destroyed at the Hostomel airport near Kiev in the first days of the Russian invasion.

The darkest sides of the Soviet experience also feature in my family history. The stories of *Holodomor* – the Great Famine of 1932–3 – which my grandmother survived as a little girl, were part of my childhood memories, along with the poems of Pushkin and Lermontov. My Red Army commissar ancestor could never meet my other great-grandfather, who was arrested as an alleged 'Polish spy' and executed in 1937 during Stalin's Great Terror. He was posthumously rehabilitated in 1956, the year Khrushchev's Thaw began. In some of the *perestroika* years, when knowledge of the extent of the crimes of Stalinism became widely discussed, I remember my grandfather looking at his father's photo and re-reading the letter in which the Soviet authorities acknowledged a 'mistake'. The state had killed his father in a fit of spy mania, for nothing. Throughout his youth, he lived with the stigma of being a 'family member of an enemy of the people', which broke his career. Nevertheless, he served this state in the military. He died suddenly in 1990 as the Soviet order was rapidly collapsing. My grandmother wondered what he would have thought about what happened next.

When the Soviet Union fell, there was no reversion to a 'natural' Ukrainianization, even under an independent Ukrainian state. Government bodies, the education system and some of the media were Ukrainianized; informal communication tended to be conducted in whichever language was convenient or predominant – Russian in the more urbanized and industrialized southeastern regions, Ukrainian in the less urbanized western and central regions. The commercial sector had little interest in switching to Ukrainian, since Russian-language cultural production could be sold to almost the entire post-Soviet Russian-speaking world. This is why so many Ukrainian media and celebrities, including future president Volodymyr Zelenskyi, produced and performed primarily or even exclusively in Russian. The Russian market was simply bigger than the Ukrainian one.

Ukrainianization was limited because the post-Soviet transformation turned out to be de-modernizing rather than modernizing, with no new vector of development to replace a Soviet project which had itself been stagnating by the 1970s (see Chapter 5). There was no alternative 'post-Soviet' way forward, only three decades of gradual degradation, and then the bloodiest war on the European continent for decades. In pre-Euromaidan polls, the majority of Ukrainians would typically say that the USSR had been rather a good thing. In retrospect, the post-Stalin Soviet years were the best period in the history of the present-day Ukrainian territories, if we care first and foremost about the lives of the masses.

In the post-Soviet period, amid constant social crisis, language and ethnonational identity became markers of political polarization. There is a tendency to see the regional cleavage in Ukrainian politics as almost an ethnic conflict between Ukrainian speakers and Russian speakers. This, however, is an essentializing, retrospective interpretation. Although it took on a more ethnonational dimension as the crisis escalated, what lay behind Ukraine's 'regional' cleavage was a class conflict.[4] The 'Western' and 'Eastern' political camps were deeply asymmetrical in terms of the social classes they sought to represent and in their political capacities.

The political capitalists – the 'oligarchs' who captured the commanding heights of the economy and the state, whom I discuss in Chapter 8 – were the camp of status quo, post-Soviet stagnation, while the 'Western' camp promised integration into neoliberal globalization. The agenda of the 'Western' camp reflected the interests of the professional middle classes. Excluded from political capitalism, they aspired to the role of comprador bourgeoisie allied with transnational capital. The latter would benefit from the enforcement of 'transparency' and 'anti-corruption', thus eliminating the main competitive advantages of Ukraine's political capitalists. The 'Western' camp was also joined by those sections of workers who were integrated into EU markets primarily as migrant workers. But the prospect of Western capitalist competition repelled other large sections of Ukrainian workers, especially employees of the big post-Soviet industries and the public sector, to whom the 'Eastern' camp could offer at least some stability in the midst of the post-Soviet collapse, and who passively supported its rule without any enthusiasm for it.

My father adapted to the post-Soviet changes, even though he had to leave behind a collapsing science sector in order to feed our family. My mother had to take several short-term jobs after leaving the Institute of Cybernetics, while also devoting herself to my sister and me. Overall, we survived the disastrous 1990s better than many Ukrainian families. I was able to benefit from a high-quality education at an elite Russian-language school, a Soviet holdover, which in the 1990s reproduced the cultural if not the economic capital of intellectuals. The reading circle of a technical intelligentsia family also played its part. Soviet science fiction, with its powerful vision of a utopian future and exploration of social and ethical issues, was crucial in developing my worldview. My parents had moved too far to the right of the political spectrum to pass on to me any irrational nostalgia for the past. What interested me was the possibility of a radically different and humane *future* of unlimited progress in taking control of natural and social forces. The movement towards that future was at the heart of the universal appeal of the Bolshevik revolution. Even faded, this vision of progress marked the worldview of the last Soviet generation.

Feeling inclined towards the social sciences, I did not follow my father's path into physics and mathematics, but chose to study at the Kiev-Mohyla Academy – a peculiar and remarkable project founded immediately after Ukraine's independence as a wannabe elite university that would combine the practices of a Western liberal arts education with the Ukrainianizing agenda of nationalist intellectuals primarily trained in the humanities. The Mohyla promised a modern education in the social sciences. Perhaps naively, I believed that in order to change society, one must first try to understand it.

From a student's perspective, the nationalist agenda at Mohyla manifested itself in the use of Ukrainian as the language of education, some pathos-laden speeches by the university administration and the views of some lecturers. Mohyla's students and faculty were, on average, more politicized than in other Ukrainian universities; they were also more internationalized, thanks in part to an emphasis on good English skills and stronger ties and exchanges with Western academia. Within this politicized milieu, a relatively small but vocal 'new left' emerged, fuelled by disillusionment with the first *maidan*, the 'Orange Revolution' of 2004. As a young lecturer at Mohyla, I actively participated in its development.

These Ukrainian *Kulturträger* won a narrow 'left' niche in middle-class civil society. They also provided 'Ukrainian voices' for certain progressive segments of the international public. But the activism in this milieu was on the whole a disappointing experience, and I reflected a lot on its problems and limitations.[3] The new left did more than simply oppose the 'old left' – nostalgically pro-Soviet, geopolitically pro-Russian, culturally conservative, not always consistently anti-oligarchic and represented primarily by the Communist Party of Ukraine (see Chapter 1). Emphasizing such oppositions indeed helped to gain us greater acceptance among the pro-Western national-liberals. At the same, it reaffirmed our distance from the majority of our people, who remained passive and atomized. I believed that overcoming this self-marginalizing dynamic required us to position ourselves *against* bourgeois civil society and appeal directly to the masses – who, thanks to the post-Soviet legacy, were potentially sympathetic to many radical ideas on economics, politics and ideology, and were not properly represented by anyone in politics or the public sphere.

For over thirty years, the Ukrainian nationalist intelligentsia had been advancing a very specific project of Ukrainian modernity. Its two main components were a rejection of Soviet modernization and an anti-Russian articulation of Ukrainian national identity. These intellectuals sought to draw an equivalence between everything Ukrainian (in their specific articulation) and everything modern, while on the other hand they hoped to associate everything backward with everything Soviet and Russian. In effect, they sought to reverse the symbolic hierarchy that identified Ukrainian with backwardness, which they feared existed behind the screen of the Soviet internationalist project. Now 'Ukrainian' should be seen as young, metropolitan, cosmopolitan, fluent in English, stylish, mobile, liberal, well-educated, successful. The 'Soviet' and 'Russian', on the other hand, had to become old, conservative, provincial, rigid, clinging to dying industries, poorly or inadequately educated, in bad taste, losers.

This polarization did not require complete homogeneity. After all, modernity is also about free rational debate. The fulfilment of Ukrainian modernity required 'Ukrainian feminists', 'Ukrainian liberals', 'Ukrainian leftists' – as well as Ukrainian rightists. Of course there should be discussion of the nationalist crimes of World War II (with the obligatory disclaimer that the Soviets were worse). Of course there should be concern about right-wing violence today (with obligatory disclaimers that it benefited Putin). And so on and so on. But at the critical moments when these discussions could really matter politically, and not just appease the 'enlightened' conscience, all the red lines were strictly enforced, and you had to get back in line. Or get in trouble.

I was so much like these people. We had so much in common in our biographies. We went through the same universities, the same scholarships, the same programmes, the same civil-society institutions, the same conferences. We spoke the same languages. But I had not begun to think like them. My peer group often reacted to this with hatred. In one trashing of me by nationalist intellectuals, I was portrayed as a danger to the dear cause of the 'Ukrainian nation-building project'. It was not because of what I wrote: they typically did not engage in any substantive discussion. And regardless of what I could possibly write, there were so much stronger forces in the media and politics that any imaginable 'threat' I posed was negligible. No, it was certainly not what I *did* that threatened the nationalist cause, but, I think, simply the *existence* of people like me. We could challenge the national-liberals as social equals in forums. We were an unwanted nuisance to their monopoly. Not really traitors to an imagined community, but traitors to a real existing social group. Class traitors, not national traitors.

Here was the real hatred. We were Ukrainian and modern, but not like them. Soviet Ukrainians who could have become comprador intellectuals in a peripheralizing country, but refused this role. We resisted their collective gaslighting. That is why there was no rational engagement, only denial, silence, rejection, cancelling. One could write thousands of words against Russian imperialism and yet still be called a 'troubadour of the empire'. One could literally say 'I hate Putin' and still be accused of spreading Russian propaganda. Our intellectuals were not rated as intellectuals. Our scholarship was not scholarship but 'political activism'. The political repression against us was not political repression, because threats and violence allegedly never occurred. We were simply not allowed to exist, because, if we did exist, the specific articulation of modernity and backwardness in Ukraine would no longer work. Whatever we did, we could not simply *be*.

We were potential embryos of an alternative Ukrainian modernity, one that could build an 'organic' representation for Soviet Ukrainians – for what they were, not for what they were 'supposed' to become in the view of nationalist intellectuals; that is, to become like them or to disappear altogether (at least from Ukraine's public sphere). We could offer an alternative for Ukraine that could also be more appealing globally (see Chapter 9) and in line with future trends, or at least with what more and more young people around the world would prefer as their future.

Why didn't it work out this way? Many have compared the post-Soviet conflicts with the collapse of empires of the past: new contested borders were drawn; ethnonational groups that were part of the imperial majority became minorities in the new states; groups that were formerly oppressed minorities were given opportunities for revenge. These comparisons are typically blind to social class and revolutionary dynamics, which provide a very different perspective. For example, the political crises and conflicts that followed the collapse of the great European empires after World War I were fundamentally different to those that followed the demise of the multinational Soviet Union. The post-Soviet crisis was the terminal crisis of a social revolution, not an *ancien régime*. The new nationalisms of a hundred years ago blossomed in the context of modernization, not de-modernization. The 1920s and '30s were a period of intense politicization, when organized revolutionary workers fought against no less committed and organized fascist counter-revolutionaries. The post-Soviet years, by contrast, were a period of atomization, of general apathy, disturbed only by short-term *maidan* mobilizations. In sum, the post– World War I crisis was a stalemate of strengthening social forces. The post-Soviet crisis was a stalemate of mutual weakness.

As noted above, the pro-Western intellectual and civic elites in post-Soviet Ukraine could offer nothing comparable to Soviet modernization. The majority of Ukrainians did not buy their dubious promises that they too could join the global middle class. But the Russian elite's offer was even less attractive. They typically compensated for their weakness in soft power with hard power. But even when they resorted to escalating coercion, they exposed their profound weaknesses. There were three critical moments when the Ukrainian majority broke away from Russia, ending up further removed from its orbit on each occasion. Each of these moments was related to the failure or mid-course correction of military coercion initiated by the Russian elite. Ukrainians responded to the failed coup in Moscow in August 1991 by voting for independence, only eight months after having voted to preserve the Soviet Union. In response to Russia's annexation of Crimea and the start of the war in Donbass in 2014, support for Russia-led reintegration projects became limited to a small minority in Ukraine, whereas they had previously been able to claim a majority or at least a plurality (see Chapter 7). The full-scale invasion in 2022 provoked the strongest anti-Russian consolidation in Ukraine's history.

These massive reactions to Russian coercion were purely negative in nature – rejections of what Russia was doing, rather than support for the West or for Ukrainian ethnonationalism. However, it was the 'Western' camp that was able to seize the opportunity of these negative shocks to advance the positive substance of its agenda. This happened because of the profound class and political asymmetries between the 'Western' and 'Eastern' camps. The political capitalists of the 'Eastern' camp did not develop their own civil society and Soviet Ukrainians remained too atomized to build their organic representation from below. Their plebeian 'anti-maidans' were never a match for the *maidan* protests they were responding to (see Chapters 1 and 2). If Volodymyr Zelenskyi's landslide victory over Petro Poroshenko in 2019 – after the incumbent ran on an aggressive nationalist programme – offered a last hope, this was dashed by the 2022 invasion.

As a result of the failure to develop and defend a pluralist nation-building project that would 'organically' grow from the Soviet Ukraine, a large group of Ukrainians is now becoming the object of assimilation policies, squeezed between the 'Western' nation-building projects of Ukrainian bourgeois civil society and Putin's nostrum of 'one and the same people'. In the notorious 2021 essay 'On the Historical Unity of Russians and Ukrainians', Putin articulated the Ukrainian–Russian distinction as a difference of regional-cultural variety within the same 'people' as a political unit. However, there is in fact less of a *cultural* difference between the population of the urbanized and mostly Russian-speaking southeastern Ukraine and the Russians, and more of a *political* difference. The urban culture of the late Soviet period, with its largely homogeneous cuisine throughout the USSR, typical references and jokes from literature and cinema, rituals and holidays, is far more relevant to them than the pre-modern ethnic traditions of Ukrainian and Russian villages. If some of the previously Russian-speaking Ukrainians switched to Ukrainian as a reaction to the invasion, it was clearly a political choice for them, not determined by their ethnic identity. The people feel more connected to the national imagined community of Ukraine, and less to Putin's, even if they have a different vision of the nation than the speakers of the 'Western' camp. In 2016, only 26 per cent of Ukrainians agreed with the statement that Ukrainians and Russians are 'one and the same people', although 51 per cent agreed that Ukrainians and Russians are different but 'brotherly people'.[5] Both figures are likely to have fallen dramatically after 2022.

For the 'Western' camp, the weak *cultural* difference of some Ukrainians from Russians has always been a *political* threat. It was seen not only as legitimizing Russian expansionism, but also as a threat to their elitist ersatz-modernization project. Quite early after the Russian missiles hit Ukrainian soil and Russian troops crossed the border, the national-liberal intellectuals understood that this was not only a threat, but also an opportunity for 'knife solutions' – a radical, uncompromising transformation of the whole country in their image and likeness on a scale that was impossible before: the war helps to silence the voices of discontent.[6] The substance of 'decolonization' (see Chapter 9) was not the building of a stronger sovereign state with a robust public sector – one that would contradict transnational capital, their crucial partner. Rather, it was the eradication of anything related to Russia or the Soviet Union from the Ukrainian public sphere, including the removal of Russian-language books from libraries, the ban on teaching Russian in schools, even in predominantly Russian-speaking cities like Odessa, and even a ridiculously obscurantist attempt (which passed the first reading in the Ukrainian parliament) to ban the citation of Russian and Russian-language sources in science and education. Add to this the banning of political parties, including some of Ukraine's oldest, such as the Socialist and Communist parties, which have represented the 'Eastern' camp for decades, and further repression of popular opposition media and bloggers stigmatized as 'pro-Russian', even when they expressed no sympathy for the invasion (see Chapter 6). Ironically, the result is similar to the situation of Ukrainians in the pre-revolutionary Russian Empire: not so much discriminated against as individuals, but prohibited from expressing a distinct collective identity that would be seen as treasonous and repressed.

In Ukraine, we can't be Soviet anymore. In Russia, it does not look like we can be Ukrainians.

Soviet Ukrainians were the product of a social revolution; its degradation destroyed them as a political community. First, the late Soviet and post-Soviet leadership became seen as nothing more than a corrupt, self-serving elite. The atomized masses responded with frequent but poorly organized and amorphous protests that, when successful, only reproduced and intensified the underlying crisis. Unlike social revolutions, the *maidans* did not bring radical transformations in favour of the popular classes; they typically only increased social inequality. The *maidan* revolutions did not even build a stronger state but only destabilized the existing one, allowing domestic and transnational elite rivals to seize the opportunity to advance their interests and agendas. The post-Soviet elite responded only with more coercion, which eventually escalated into war (see how it worked out with the successful repression of the 2020 uprising in Belarus in Chapter 4). This set the stage for the flourishing not of developmental national ideologies but of regressive neo-tribalist identities. There was no strong force from below to counteract this dynamic. The processes of the escalating crisis of hegemony are universal, but their manifestations in the post-Soviet space are of a rather unique magnitude.

The decomposition of a political community is the ultimate endpoint of these crisis trends. Divided by frontlines and borders, some volunteering, some being mobilized by force, some collaborating, some fleeing abroad, some trying to maintain a normal life and work in their hometowns, some simply trying to survive, taking different positions on the war (who even cares what 'Ukrainian voices' who speak from Donetsk or Sevastopol think?), lacking our political and public representatives, with limited space for expression, with broken ties and suppressed discussions; is there even a common name, a claimed identity for all of us now? It is easy to pretend that we have never even existed, at most a dead-end branch from the main line of Ukrainian nation-building. But one can be sure that without a new cycle of modernizing development in Ukraine, Soviet Ukrainians will not be fully assimilated. The political communication required to define our common identity, interests and collective actions in relation to Ukraine, and the states where we will end up, may start again.

The revolutionary project initiated by the Bolsheviks a hundred years ago has lost its embeddedness in the national communities where it once took root. For the contemporary left, this should mean not a break with the project of progress, rationality and universal emancipation, but rather the search for a political (and perhaps no longer national) community in which our efforts could be more effectively applied. Any new social revolution would learn from the Soviet one as much as the Bolsheviks learned from the

French Revolution of 1789 – understanding its limits and acknowledging its (sometimes unjustifiable) mistakes, but also registering and building on its achievements.

Could Ukraine again be a core part of a social-revolutionary movement? The extent of the ethnonationalist and anti-communist reformatting of the country's politics, society and ideology may leave no hope for this in the foreseeable future. But consider how dramatically the memory of the World War II has changed over time. Who could have imagined in 1945, after the Nazi war of extermination and enslavement on the Eastern Front, which murdered between one-sixth and one-quarter of the entire civilian population of Ukraine, that the descendants of the survivors would fight using German tanks against Russians on the very same battlefields where they had fought in the Red Army against German tanks, and would do so while demolishing the remaining monuments to their heroic ancestors? It is unlikely to be the final ironic twist of Ukrainian history.

2014

Recap of Events

The political system that emerged in Ukraine was from the outset more pluralistic than those of, say, Russia, Kazakhstan or Belarus. This is often thought to be rooted in the country's proverbial 'east/west' regional cleavage, visible in electoral outcomes from the 1990s onwards.[1] Any candidate who won the presidential elections would not be seen as legitimate by almost half the population, who would immediately voice strong opposition to him. But it seems that this 'regional' polarization was mainly a Ukraine-specific articulation of the central class conflict in the post-Soviet world: that between, on the one hand, the professional middle classes allied with transnational capital and, on the other, local political capitalists (colloquially known as 'oligarchs') who could only rely on the passive consent of a segment of the working class, mainly in heavy industry and the public sector.

Among the Ukrainian presidents, Leonid Kuchma (president from 1994–2005) and, later, Viktor Yanukovych (2010–14) were the most prominent political representatives of the latter camp. With the state's assistance, the notorious 'oligarchs' acquired old Soviet industries at fire-sale prices, and then made huge fortunes not so much by investing or upgrading as by using them to make quick money, and shifting their capital to Cyprus or other offshore havens. For many years, Kuchma and Yanukovych were also able to balance on the question of whether to integrate into Europe's economic sphere or Russia's, moving neither to the West nor the East. This shielded Ukraine's oligarchs, preventing them from being swallowed by stronger Russian or European competitors.

Unable to steal the elections in 2004, Yanukovych quickly recovered to win the presidency in 2010. Despite signing a 'Platform of Practical Activities' with the Communist Party which included an extensive list of relatively progressive policies on socioeconomic issues, support for the Russian-speaking population, economic integration with Russia and political reform, Yanukovych quickly reneged on his promises and proceeded to concentrate political power and lucrative economic assets in his informal 'Family' clan, betting (on the advice of Paul Manafort) that steps towards Western integration, particularly Ukraine's association with the European Union (EU), would help him get re-elected. By the time Yanukovych took office, Ukraine had already been hit harder by the global financial crisis than any other post-Soviet state: there was a slump in prices for Ukrainian-produced goods, especially metals. This made it very difficult for Yanukovych to balance the interests of different classes and groups in Ukrainian society with those of the oligarchic elite, and deliver on the promised 'stability' – the main selling point of authoritarian leaders in the region after the post-Soviet economic collapse.

Yanukovych's downfall was triggered by his announcement on 21 November 2013 that he would be suspending negotiations on an EU Association Agreement. The terms of the International Monetary Fund (IMF) credit that the government was negotiating also played a role: the IMF demanded a rise in gas consumption prices for the population, wage freezes and significant budget cuts, all of which would be a blow for the poor classes of Ukraine. Not so much for the middle classes; defined mainly by consumption levels, these amount to no more than 10–15 per cent of the population, and were concentrated in the biggest cities, working either for the oligarchs' industries or in the offices of Western corporations. The 'political' part of the EU treaty was very short and vague; more important was the free-trade zone with the EU, although there was little public discussion of its consequences for the various groups of Ukrainian society. Later studies concluded that it would harm the most advanced parts of Ukrainian industry, concentrated mainly in the southeastern regions.[2]

In the beginning, the Euromaidan movement mostly consisted of middle-class Kievans and students, driven by a European ideology – a 'European dream', offering the hope of some kind of breakthrough to a better society. But there was also a strong anti-Russian, nationalist component. After an attempted crackdown in the early morning of 30 November 2013, people started to build barricades in the centre of Kiev and the protesters moved in and occupied administrative buildings. Far-right militants were quite active in these occupations – they led the seizure of the City State Administration building on Khreshchatyk, the main street in Kiev, and established their headquarters there. It was also far-rightists who attacked the presidential administration on 1 December; there were violent clashes with riot police for several hours, resulting in hundreds of people being injured.

After a month and a half of occupation of Kiev's central square and a political stalemate, there was further violence when the parliament passed a package of repressive new laws on 16 January. The confrontation with the police escalated to an armed civil conflict on 18 February when the government refused to concede on constitutional reform. In the west of Ukraine, protesters started to attack police stations and raid their arsenals, getting hold of guns in large quantities. In some places the police shot at protesters, but in many areas they left without offering much resistance. Dozens were killed on 20 February in the centre of Kiev, many of them by snipers whose identities remain undetermined. The ruling Party of Regions faction quickly began to dissolve, and many deputies joined the opposition. This transformed the balance of forces in parliament: there was now an opposition majority. An agreement for a transition of power to a 'national unity' government signed by Yanukovych and opposition representatives proved short-lived. Yanukovych fled the capital on the evening of 21 February in the futile hope of falling back on the support of elites in southeastern Ukraine, while the opposition took power in Kiev, claiming dereliction of duty by the president. An interim government of the oligarchic opposition parties, including radical nationalists from the *Svoboda* party, took office. The US and EU approved the change of government, though it wasn't in accord with the recently signed transition agreement. The incoming prime minister, Arseniy Yatsenyuk, a former banker, signed the political provisions of the EU Association Agreement on 21 March.

· Moscow decided on the annexation of Crimea soon after southeastern Ukraine failed to rally behind Yanukovych. The annexation crisis boosted the domestic legitimacy of the new Yatsenyuk government. Some people began to volunteer for the army and the newly established National Guard, and there were mass rallies in support of Ukraine's sovereignty and territorial integrity. At the same time, however, Ukraine quickly began to polarize. There had been 'Anti-Maidan' rallies in the east – Kharkov, Donetsk, Lugansk, Dnepropetrovsk – since late 2013, though these were largely orchestrated by Yanukovych and the ruling Party of Regions. After Yanukovych was toppled, the mobilizations in the east became more intense – especially with the Russian intervention in Crimea – and acquired a grassroots dimension. In some places, leftist parties and organizations played a prominent role in the Anti-Maidan protests along with Russian nationalist groups. Separatist groups began to seize local administrative buildings. In early April, Russian volunteers, well-equipped, organized the armed seizure of Sloviansk.

The presidential election of 25 May 2014 was won by Petro Poroshenko, billionaire owner of the Roshen confectionery business, who had swung back and forth between the 'pro-Western' and 'pro-Russian' camps in Ukrainian politics. One of the founders of the Party of Regions, he had supported the earlier 2004 Orange revolution that blocked Yanukovych's original (and fraudulent) tilt at the presidency, but later took a ministerial office in Yanukovych's post-2010 government. Poroshenko had supported the Maidan and was one of the politicians who appeared most frequently on the stage in Independence Square. His attempt to retake Donbass militarily during the summer of 2014 was thwarted by the covert intervention of the Russian Army, leading to the signing of the Minsk Accords, which were never properly implemented. Domestically, instead of channelling the admittedly rather vague social content of the Euromaidan revolution, Poroshenko turned to a nationalist agenda focused on historical memory, language and religion. In foreign policy, he amended the Constitution to state that Ukraine's 'strategic course' was now full membership of NATO as well as the EU, overriding the country's previous tradition of non-alignment. In 2019, Volodymyr Zelenskyi, a TV comedian with zero political experience, prevailed over Poroshenko in a landslide election.

1

Ukraine Protests Are No Longer
Just about Europe

22 January 2014

There is little doubt that Viktor Yanukovych's rule is corrupt. It stands for the interests of the richest few in Ukraine's highly unequal society and is responsible for the brutal suppression of opposition. The majority of protesting Ukrainians hope for a just, fair and democratic society, even if naively connecting this hope to an idealized 'Europe'.

Yet Euromaidan, Ukraine's pro-EU protest movement, has still not become a point of conflict between the Ukrainian government and Ukrainian society as a whole. According to the polls, support for Euromaidan is heavily concentrated in the western and central regions, while Ukrainians living in the east and the south of the country overwhelmingly disapprove. After mass violence and clashes with the police started on Sunday, in which a leading role was played by a far-right network of groups called Right Sector, there is no doubt that people in the eastern and southern regions would condemn the protests even more. This is unfortunate, because the agenda of the protest has shifted from a desire to be associated with Europe to the struggle against the police state after parliament ripped up the Constitution and rushed through laws restricting, among others, the freedom of peaceful assembly and freedom of speech.

The Right Sector militants did not appear from nowhere, although many media and liberal protesters preferred to ignore their existence. They were active participants in the protest from the very beginning, interested not so much in European association as the 'national revolution'. They efficiently infiltrated the volunteer guards of the tent camps.

On 1 December, they were the main force behind the violent attack near the presidential administration, contrary to the popular version that blamed government provocateurs. When, last Sunday, Vitali Klitschko, the most probable next president of Ukraine according to the polls, tried to stop clashes with police, he was booed. Many protesters, who could not imagine themselves throwing stones and Molotovs at the police line before, joined the violence of the extreme right, frustrated at the lack of progress after coming each Sunday to listen to the same talks from opposition leaders.

Yet those who may be thrilled with the illusion of an all-national revolt are forgetting that this is another step in the normalization of the far right. Right Sector has already efficiently mainstreamed its slogans ('Glory to Ukraine! Glory to the heroes!', 'Glory to the nation! Death to enemies!', 'Ukraine above everything!'). We must not forget that these are people with sometimes overtly neo-Nazi ideas who would eagerly pass even more repressive laws, but only against other, ethnically defined enemies.

Several thousand people are participating in the violent clashes but, outside the two central squares and several neighbouring blocks, everyday life in Kiev is going on as usual.

This week, though, riot police demonstrated that they can restore control over the streets in a few minutes and that they are ready to open fire against protesters – two have been killed with gunshots, as of midday on Wednesday.

What could be the alternative to this dead-end of senseless rallies without action and no less senseless violence? The negotiations that started between the opposition and some representatives of the government seem to be only an attempt to calm down the protesters. However, on Monday, students at Kiev-Mohyla Academy, one of the best universities in Ukraine, started an indefinite strike against the police state laws, aiming to entirely stop teaching in their university and initiate political strikes on other campuses and workers' strikes. If they succeed, they could show the way to a non-violent but still radical and efficient way to bring down Yanukovych's government.[1]

28 February 2014

Two popular labels are being ascribed to events in Ukraine: it was either a democratic – or even social – revolution, or a right-wing – or even neo-Nazi – coup. In fact, both characterizations are wrong.[2] What we have seen is a mass rebellion, overwhelmingly supported in western and central Ukraine but without majority support in the eastern and southern regions, leading to a change of political elites. But there are no prospects for democratic, radical change, at least under the new government.

Why was it neither a social nor a democratic revolution? Some of the demands of the Maidan movement have been implemented. For example, the notorious Berkut regiment – the riot police who killed most of the dead protesters – was disbanded and the most odious of the former Yanukovych officials have been sacked. However, this does not mean the start of systematic democratic change, or that the new government is in any way going to challenge the root of pervasive corruption in Ukraine: poverty and inequality. Moreover, it is likely only to aggravate these problems, putting the burden of the economic crisis on the shoulders of Ukraine's poor, not on the rich Ukrainian oligarchs. The socioeconomic demands of the Maidan movement have been replaced with the neoliberal agenda of the new government. The cabinet, approved on Thursday, consists mainly of neoliberals and nationalists. The official programme of action it presented to parliament declares the need for 'unpopular decisions' on prices and tariffs and its readiness to fulfil all the conditions of the loan from the International Monetary Fund (IMF). The IMF's requirements to freeze wages and hike gas prices were among the reasons why the former government suspended negotiations on an EU Association Agreement. No wonder so many people are calling the new administration the 'government of suicides'. It is not hard to forecast mass disappointment with these antisocial policies and a collapse of the currency, further impoverishing ordinary Ukrainians.

The far right has also achieved a major breakthrough in the government. Some commentators have warned that their level of representation in the new Ukrainian government is unparalleled in Europe. The xenophobic Svoboda party controls the posts of deputy prime minister, ministers of defence, ecology, agriculture and the prosecutor general's office. Andriy Parubiy, one of the founders of the Social-National Party of Ukraine and a former leader of its paramilitary youth organization, who later joined the moderate Batkivshchyna party and efficiently commanded self-defence forces in Maidan, is now the head of the National Security and Defense Council.

At the same time, the protest does not fit the classical definition of a coup: a well-planned armed seizure of power. The Maidan movement, particularly its paramilitary arm, was hardly controlled by the parliamentary parties. In fact, these parties were regularly trying to pacify the movement, and urging compromises with Yanukovych, albeit without much success.

What is most worrying is that the new government cannot control the infamous Right Sector. Its members are now popular heroes, the vanguard of the victorious 'revolution'. They have guns captured from police departments in the western regions and now, after Yanukovych's toppling, are demanding that the revolution continue against 'corrupt democracy' and liberalism. The liberals celebrating their decisiveness and crucial role in the Maidan movement are now discovering the right's reactionary ideas. Recently, the press secretary of the Right Sector gave an interview saying 'we need to tell Europe the right way to go' and save it from the 'terrible situation' of 'total liberalism', where people don't go to church and are tolerant of lesbian, gay, bisexual and transgender rights.

It is too soon for the Right Sector to move against the new government – it lacks the support. But the group may lead a new insurrection in the event of a rapid and deepening economic crisis. In the absence of any strong leftist force in Ukraine, social grievances will be whipped up by right-wing populists. At the same time, the leading role of radical Ukrainian nationalists in a potential new 'social Maidan' will preclude any all-national movement against the ruling class, with mass participation from the east and the south of culturally divided Ukraine. Moreover, they even amplify separatist attitudes and attempts of pro-Russian provocations, as we have seen in Crimea. Full-scale civil war, although not inevitable, is a real threat now.

In this situation, the best policy for the West would be to insist on the peaceful resolution of the inter-regional conflicts in Ukraine, taking a strong position against participation of the far right in the new government and uncontrolled rightist paramilitaries on the streets. Last, but not least, the West could offer unconditional help to Ukraine by cancelling its foreign debt – a popular demand raised by many progressive movements all over the world.

15 April 2014

I have little doubt that Russian security services were in some way involved in the recent escalation of violence in several towns in eastern Ukraine. The seizures of administrative buildings on 12 April were well coordinated between different towns, the armed men were well equipped and showed high levels of military training. This does not necessarily mean that Russian special operations units are directly taking part; those men could be former Ukrainian riot police officers, many of whom fled to Crimea and Russia to escape punishment from the new government. But all of this does not preclude the fact that the planned provocation happened in the context of mass, grassroots, self-organized social protests in eastern Ukrainian regions which started against the new government after former president Viktor Yanukovych was toppled.

The Maidan movement has never had majority support in the eastern and southern regions of Ukraine. After it succeeded in toppling the government, many people were scared and outraged by the exaggerated pictures they saw on television of violent clashes in Kiev, armed paramilitary groups including many far-right elements controlling the streets, attacks on Lenin's monuments, and the far-right Svoboda party being included in the new government. Many people in the east call it the 'Kiev junta' and disapprove of its actions. Of course, there is a large degree of irrational fear driving the protesters, especially concerning the overstated problem of Russian-language discrimination. But it would be hypocritical to employ double standards. Just as Maidan was not a 'revolution', anti-Maidan is not a 'counter-revolution' either. Maidan was called a 'revolution of dignity', but people in eastern Ukraine are also proudly talking about their dignity, regional identity, historical memory, Soviet heroes and language.

The supporters of anti-Maidans in the east are no more irrational than Maidan protesters who were hoping for the European dream but gained (quite expectedly) a neoliberal government, IMF-required austerity measures and increasing prices. In the eastern Ukrainian protests, 'Russia' – with its higher wages and pensions – plays the same role of utopian aspiration as 'Europe' played for the Maidan protesters. The economic situation in Ukraine continues to deteriorate and the national currency has lost more than 50 per cent of its value in two months, so the protesters in the Donetsk region are talking more about the socioeconomic problems the Ukrainian state has not been able to solve for twenty-three years: collapsed enterprises, unemployment and low wages. They demand nationalization and decent rewards for their labour.

It will sound paradoxical for those who celebrated grassroots self-organization in the Maidan, but the anti-Maidan protests in eastern Ukraine are even more grassroots, decentralized, network-type and leaderless at the moment. Neither the Party of Regions nor the Communist Party of Ukraine plays the same role of political representation for anti-Maidan as the three former opposition parties did for Maidan. The so-called 'representative of southeastern Ukraine', the former governor of the Kharkov region Mykhailo Dobkin, whom Russia was going to invite to the negotiations with the EU and US on an equal basis with the Kiev government, was violently booed by protesters in Lugansk. Equally, they do not trust the oligarchic elite of eastern Ukrainian origin; or the wealthiest person in Ukraine, Rinat Akhmetov, who has taken on a peacemaker role; or the new Donetsk governor Serhiy Taruta. And they do not want the discredited and corrupt Yanukovych back. The social base of the protest seems to be more plebeian, poorer and less educated than that of the Maidan; we see more workers and pensioners and not so many intellectuals and highly educated professionals who would help to formulate clear demands and defend them in the media. This is precisely why these protests can be so easily influenced from the outside. It is not difficult to intervene, provoke and manipulate a decentralized revolt of scared people to serve Russian interests.

The anti-Maidan protests cannot be supported wholeheartedly and without reservation. Like Maidan their causes are diverse. Some people support joining Russia, some support more local autonomy within the Ukrainian state. Russian far-right nationalists, who are no better than the Ukrainian nationalist Svoboda or Right Sector, participate in the protests together with leftist organizations. The public in eastern and southern Ukraine is split. At the same time as anti-Maidan rallies and seizures, demonstrations in support of the new government and a united Ukraine take place.

Even if from an abstract point of view a demand for federalization and the direct election of the region's governors sounds democratic, in the Ukrainian reality it would instead give more powers to local 'big men' rather than lead to a strong local self-government. And like in western Ukraine during the final stages of the Maidan rebellion, the local Donetsk police are now sabotaging the government's orders and are often allowed to take control of the buildings and weapons without much resistance, sometimes even taking the side of the protesters.

Rather than constructing necessarily hypocritical justifications as to why military suppression of some armed protesters is better than military suppression of other armed protesters, why the pro-Ukrainian far right is better than the pro-Russian far right, why the Ukrainian neoliberal government is better than the Russian neoliberal government, or why we are ready to fight Russian imperialism but ready to accept Western imperialist interests in Ukraine, it would be better to support the progressive wings of both Maidan and anti-Maidan, and try to unite them against the Ukrainian ruling class and against all nationalisms and imperialisms, focusing instead on shared demands for social justice.

13 November 2014

Pro-Russian supporters use the term 'fascist junta' to criticize the Ukrainian government. This wording is not only obviously wrong from an understanding of the words 'fascism' and 'junta', but has also been detrimental to peace in Ukraine by fuelling the civil war. If your country is governed by a fascist junta, any progressive person should take arms and fight it. But despite the hypocritical instrumentalization of the Russian propaganda, the Ukrainian authorities and mainstream opinion in Ukraine continue to show unacceptable ignorance of the danger from the far right and even openly neo-Nazi forces, cooperating with them in elections and allowing them to take positions within law enforcement.

The major Ukrainian far-right party, Svoboda, did not get into parliament in recent elections, falling only 0.3 per cent short of the required minimum of 5 per cent. It was not able to repeat its success of 2012, when it got more than 10 per cent by exploiting its image as the most radical party running against the former president Viktor Yanukovych, in contrast to the discredited moderate opposition. The party's support might have been boosted by anti-Yanukovych feelings, but it shouldn't be wholly dismissed as a protest vote; the 4.7 per cent gain is much higher than the 0.8 per cent seen in 2007 during the last parliamentary elections before his rule. Besides, the Right Sector, made up of fringe ultra-nationalist groups before the mass street violence began in Kiev in January, was able to form a party and get 1.8 per cent, obviously taking some votes from Svoboda.

It is short-sighted and formalistic to conclude that the Ukrainian far right is insignificant based on its lack of electoral success. The rhetoric of many politicians which could be called centrist or even liberal has moved significantly to the right, competing for the increasingly patriotic and even nationalist voters. There were a number of incidents of hate speech used even by top Ukrainian politicians, such as the Minister of the Interior Arsen Avakov referring to Donetsk separatists as 'colorados', a pejorative, dehumanizing label which compares them with the Colorado beetle due to their orange and black St George's ribbons.

In an increasingly nationalist political competition, the far-right parties failed to propose anything outstanding. But it does not mean they cannot do it later. Outside parliament, Svoboda (as well as the Right Sector) might well criticize the new government not only on nationalist grounds, but also by highlighting a deteriorating economic situation.

Despite the failures of far-right parties, thirteen far-right MPs have been elected to parliament in the single-member districts or in the lists of formally 'non-far-right' parties, including the Radical Party of political clown Oleg Lyashko and even the pro-presidential Petro Poroshenko Bloc. Moreover, some of the new MPs are not just far right but actual neo-Nazis. Take Andriy Biletsky, elected in a single-member district in Kiev with support from the People's Front Party led by Arseniy Yatsenyuk. Biletsky was the head of an openly racist Patriot of Ukraine group which was involved in hate crimes against minorities, and later formed the core of the infamous Azov volunteer battalion, which uses neo-Nazi symbolism. He was celebrated as commander of the Azov battalion and assigned to the rank of lieutenant colonel in the police.

Biletsky is not the only neo-Nazi recently appointed to law enforcement bodies. In October, Vadym Troyan, another Patriot of Ukraine member and deputy commander of the Azov battalion, was appointed as the head of the police in Kiev oblast. A Kharkov human rights group called it a 'disastrous appointment'. At the same time, another infamous extreme-right politician from the Svoboda party, Yuriy Mykhalchyshyn, who once promoted Joseph Goebbels' *A Little ABC of National Socialism* and the NSDAP 25-point Programme, will head up propaganda and analysis in the Security Service of Ukraine. Allowing people with such extreme views control over positions with significant enforcement resources is an obvious danger to democracy.

But what is striking is that far-right and neo-Nazi views and connections do not seem to be problematic for either Ukrainian officials or mainstream opinion. Even the most typical line of criticism against Svoboda and the Right Sector expressed by liberal-minded people is inherently flawed. They may agree that the far right is dangerous, but they argue that the danger is that its provocative actions and statements can be exploited by Russian media to further discredit Ukraine. In this twisted logic, the far right is criticised first of all for putting its partisan interests above Ukraine's national interests. In other words, it is criticised not for being anti-democratic, reactionary, xenophobic and for propagating discriminatory ideas, but for not being nationalist enough. Even in critical discussions around the far-right appointments to high positions within law enforcement, there seem to be more worries about Ukraine's international image than about what neo-Nazis can do against political opponents and minorities and the dangerous resources they might accumulate.

Ukrainians have already paid a very high price for ignoring the far right. According to systematic research into protests, members of the far right were the most visibly identified political agents in the Maidan protests, from the very beginning of the movement to the overthrow of Yanukovych.[3] Moreover, they were relatively more visible in eastern and southern regions where Maidan did not have the majority support, thus pushing the local population even further away from the protest message. This was not a Russian media invention. On the contrary, it happened as a result of the preceding protest coalition of the centrist opposition parties with Svoboda. High visibility of the far right was one of the factors which prevented Maidan from growing into a truly national movement against Yanukovych, and formed the ground for the civil war.

Of course, Vladimir Putin bears a greater responsibility for this. But those Maidan supporters who consistently ignored, silenced and downplayed the significance and danger of the far right instead of decisively breaking away are also partly responsible. This tolerance has already cost Ukraine lost territories, a mass destruction of industry and infrastructure, and thousands and thousands of lives. It is necessary to break with the 'it might be beneficial for Putin' logic and start to think about what is beneficial for all the people living in Ukraine, and whether the radical nationalist ideas can fit the Ukrainian future to which we aspire.

4 September 2015

Violence erupted outside the parliament building in Kiev this week during protests against constitutional changes which could grant more autonomy to pro-Russian separatists in eastern Ukraine. Proposed by President Petro Poroshenko, these changes would decentralize power in Ukraine, allowing local self-government in 'certain districts of Donetsk and Lugansk regions', to be determined by a separate law. The proposals, supported by the US and EU, form part of a promise made in the Minsk Accords to grant 'special status' to the pro-Russian rebel-held regions to help end the ongoing conflict in eastern Ukraine. But in reality, these constitutional changes are only a distant relation to the letter of the Minsk Accords. Poroshenko's proposal is not approved by the separatists, or by the Kremlin. It does not really give any 'special status' to separatist areas, and any specific details on autonomous rule in Donbass may later be revised by a simple majority vote in Ukrainian parliament. Moreover, the so-called 'decentralization' is accompanied by a strengthening of the presidential control over local self-government via centrally assigned 'prefects' with broad powers.

The far-right Svoboda party, the Right Sector party and some of the current coalition government parties criticized the changes as a 'capitulation' to Russia, and Monday's protests turned bloody after a man – reportedly a member of a far-right battalion, called *Sich* – threw a hand grenade into a dense police line. The government reported that more than 130 law enforcement officials had been injured, and four National Guard soldiers – all young draftees – died from injuries.

The Sich battalion, created with the support of Svoboda, is one of many formed in the past year to challenge separatist rebels supported by Russia in the east of the country.

However, in an interview with Sky News on Wednesday, Poroshenko claimed Russia was in fact responsible for the deaths. The president claimed the Kremlin's ongoing 'campaign of destabilization' was to blame, despite clear indications that it was far-right nationalist supporters who were driving the clashes with the police.

Responding to the clashes, the Svoboda party claimed the violence was a planned provocation to discredit 'patriots', while pro-government groups and the liberal Ukrainian public have in turn hysterically blamed Svoboda for the deaths of the soldiers.

Rare voices from the left are now quickly reminding the liberals – in firm 'I told you so' mode – that they had warned of the dangers of prolonged cooperation with the far right at a much earlier stage, and this violence, they suggest, is the outcome.

But as usual in cases of tragedy, emotions are selective. Throwing a hand grenade into a dense crowd is hardly the worst act of violence going on in

Ukraine today. Even worse atrocities are committed almost every day in the Donbass region by 'ordinary' people from both sides of the conflict. But during war violence can become trivialized, particularly when it is far from home – and far from Kiev. However, the war takes on new meaning when an angry and armed veteran comes back feeling betrayed by the government.

It is the current government that bears more responsibility for the ongoing conflict than the Ukrainian far right and its armed groups. It is the current government that is responsible for new repressions, censorship and discriminatory measures. Though right-wing parties like Svoboda and the Right Sector were indeed prominent in the Euromaidan uprising in 2013, later increasing their resources and forming their own armed units, they have not been able so far to gather mass support behind them. Today, they merely react to the events – they're not pushing them forward. Even in the case of Monday's violence, Svoboda was just trying to win political points on the eve of local elections, hoping to give their calls of 'national betrayal' a greater platform. They are unlikely to have seriously planned an armed attack; they just weren't able to control their extremist supporters in the crowd.

Though the government has already used Monday's violence to discredit Svoboda's members as irresponsible politicos, it remains to be seen whether it will now attempt to repress the far right. But perhaps an even more pressing question is whether the government even has the capacity to suppress the right, given their growing bands of loyal armed units. As suggested by the violence in the western town of Mukachevo – where Right Sector combatants clashed with law enforcement, leaving seven dead – when the far right have several thousand armed men who can challenge the state monopoly on violence; can call for an open mutiny against the state; and still suffer almost no serious consequences, how powerful is the government really?

Frighteningly, the main alternative to our right-wing nationalist government is an ultra-right opposition. Meanwhile, as the government points fingers, the coalition is fracturing. The populist Radical Party has quit the government over the decentralization bill.

Gathering the votes in parliament for the final approval of the constitutional changes also seemed to be impossible without support from the Opposition Bloc, a successor to the pro-Yanukovych Party of Regions – a very symbolic fact that will only give more ground for the far right to attack the government for betraying the Euromaidan 'revolution'.

What may emerge in Ukrainian politics is a frightening situation, where the main alternative to a right-wing nationalist government is an ultra-right, ultra-nationalist opposition.

18 December 2015

An anti-communist hysteria is prevailing in Kiev. After banning Soviet symbols earlier this year, a court has now outlawed the Communist Party of Ukraine, preventing it from organizing and taking part in elections. The ban has been criticized by civil liberties campaigners, who say it contravenes the European Convention on Human Rights, to which Ukraine is a signatory. Under the convention, a political party cannot be banned for its symbols – rather, there must be 'proven activities' that are dangerous to the national security. But the irony is that the Communist Party of Ukraine is neither communist nor dangerous. The only things the party has in common with the determined Bolshevik revolutionaries of the past, who spared neither themselves nor others, are devotion to the Soviet symbols and appeals to empty 'Marxist-Leninist' phrases.

Ukraine's Communist Party was the most popular political party in the country during market reforms in the 1990s, but it has since degenerated into a conservative and pro-Russian rather than pro-working-class party, gradually losing its voters and elderly membership. Party leaders became a part of the bourgeois elite and invited business support for their cause. The richest woman in the previous session of Ukrainian parliament, multimillionaire Oksana Kaletnik, was a member of the communist group. After the fall of Viktor Yanukovych's government following the pro-European Maidan protests in 2014, some communist activists and local organizations did support the separatist uprising in the east of the country. However, the party leadership repeatedly stated its support for Ukrainian territorial integrity and excluded dissenters from its membership.

The party's inconsistent stance towards the war in eastern Ukraine is one of the reasons for its current crisis. It hysterically criticized the 'national fascist' regime that took over in Kiev while saying not a single critical word about Russia. Yet its statements were not backed by deeds. Communist Party leaders disappointed many former members who expected more decisive actions against the post-Maidan government of billionaire chocolate tycoon Petro Poroshenko. Combined with the loss of a large part of the pro-communist electorate in Russian and separatist-controlled Crimea and Donbass, the party failed to get into the parliament in October 2014 for the first time in its history. Despite being banned from local elections two months ago, Communist Party candidates participated under the banner of the New State party – but performed even worse than before, winning only slightly more than 1 per cent of the votes.

Now the Communist Party is simply an easy scapegoat. The Ukrainian government needs to continue the ideological war to divert attention from rising prices and austerity. In doing so, it is building political intolerance in a country already torn apart by war. The ban will not make the party stronger. This is not an organization able to close ranks, go underground and fight. It will appeal to the European Court of Human Rights (ECHR) and might well win the case – as has happened in similar situations of anti-communist repression and censorship in Eastern Europe.[4]

But the crackdowns and electoral defeats have exacerbated already deep internal divisions within the party. Recently, nineteen local leaders from southern and eastern Ukrainian organizations resigned from the central committee to protest against repression of internal dissent. They blamed a very unpopular Petro Symonenko, who has been party leader since it was founded in 1993. The left flank of Ukrainian politics is vacant for now, but it won't be for long. New 'left' political projects sponsored by oligarchs are likely to appear, trying to gather the former communist votes and some of the local membership.

On the other side, some 'pro-Ukrainian left' party will probably arise to legitimize the government in the eyes of the West.[5] It will mostly support the government's policies against Russia and Donbass separatists but will criticize it from mild social-democratic or left-liberal positions. But the genuine left should not become pawns in oligarchs' electoral games or act as the loyal whitewashers of a neoliberal-nationalist government. A new left party should be deeply embedded in Ukrainian social movements and labour unions. It should be neither pro-Kiev nor pro-Moscow but bring together ordinary people in the west and east in a fight for their shared class interests against their common enemies in Kiev, Donetsk, Moscow, Brussels and Washington. Genuine internationalism and going back to the class roots are the only ways for the new left in Ukraine. Every person who values democracy must oppose the ban of the Communist Party. It violates human rights. It adds to political hysteria. It diverts attention away from urgent problems in the Ukrainian economy.

But we have to understand the mistakes the communists made and avoid them in the reconstruction of the Ukrainian left.

2

Maidan Mythologies

On Andrew Wilson's *Ukraine Crisis: What It Means for the West* (2014)

Andrew Wilson's earlier publications on Ukraine won him a reputation as a serious historian. His first books – notably *Ukrainian Nationalism in the 1990s* (1997), *The Ukrainians* (2002) and *Ukraine's Orange Revolution* (2005) – were distinguished by three signature features. First, Wilson argued strongly that while Ukrainian nationalism was a force in the west of the country – where, bred under Austrian and Polish rule, it had mostly possessed a strong right-wing bent – it had only limited appeal in the country as a whole, due to the existence of deep regional, linguistic and ethnic historical divisions. Ukrainian 'national identity', Wilson insisted in *The Ukrainians*, was essentially a product of the Soviet era. Second, he made no bones about the fact that, since 1990, the country had had a sorry economic and political record; the state was thoroughly colonized by oligarchy, thuggery and corruption; civil society remained very weak. It was a myth, Wilson argued, that Ukraine's political culture was more tolerant, democratic and pluralist than Russia's. Third, Wilson provided detailed analysis of the various oligarchic bosses and clans, and of their rivalries. *Ukraine's Orange Revolution* offered praise for the protests of 2004 and was cautiously optimistic about the Yushchenko–Tymoshenko regime that emerged from them.

His latest book, the ill-titled *Ukraine Crisis*, constitutes a sharp break from this earlier work in direction, tone and genre. This may in part be the product of the author's transformation from historian to foreign-policy agitator: Wilson is now a senior fellow of the European Council on Foreign Relations, a lavishly funded think-tank modelled on its US homonym, which has grown since its birth in 2007 to become a large octopus in the EU aquarium. The position has allowed him a back-room role in EU diplomacy – there is a casual reference to his presence at the November 2013 Vilnius summit – and indeed *Ukraine Crisis* was partly funded by EU Commission money. The book bears the marks of this shift. Readers should not expect to find in its pages a balanced assessment of contending arguments or a systematic analysis of the available sources, followed by well-grounded conclusions. For the most part, this is a one-sided, tendentious account of Ukraine's Maidan protests of 2013–14, the Russian intervention and the civil war, heavily reliant on web-sourced information, anonymous interviews and hectic prose, pieced together to bolster a very specific political agenda. It is driven by a desire not to investigate what actually happened and why, but rather to rebut critics – from all sides – of a Western neoliberal line. The nature of Russian policy, the legitimacy of the Yanukovych government and the character of the Maidan protests are all grist to this mill.

In his introduction, Wilson insists that *Ukraine Crisis* is not 'an anti-Russian book', before proceeding to deliver exactly that. The anti-Putin message is expressed in the crudest of terms: 'The key to understanding modern Russia is to realize that it is run by some very weird people.' Wilson asserts that Russia's rulers believe their country has been 'constantly humili-ated' since 1991; this externally imposed 'humiliation' must now be avenged by restoring its Great Power status. He denies that Russia is in any way 'encircled or threatened' by NATO's expansion. His argument is that Russia was brought down by its own oligarchs, the social layer that benefited most from the fall of communism through their capture of state power and property. Some of the oligarchic groups were wealthier and luckier than others; 'Putin's friends' and the *siloviki* were able to monopolize power by removing dangerous competitors, marginalizing opponents and manipulating the population with a complex dramaturgy scripted by 'political technologists'. The latest example of this is the 'conservative values' project of 2014, an attempt to shore up a Putin majority after the opposition protests of 2011–12. For Wilson, a similar monopolization of power by Yanukovych and his allies was blocked by the Maidan protests.

Wilson devotes a good few pages to countering the argument – widely propounded by Ukrainian opponents of the Maidan – that Yanukovych was a legitimately elected president, overthrown by a violent 'coup'. He argues that Yanukovych himself was the first to break the formal rules of the game after beating Yulia Tymoshenko in the 2010 presidential election. Reputedly by bribery or threat, he secured the majority vote in parliament needed to remove Tymoshenko from the prime minister's office. Within a year of Yanukovych taking office, Ukraine's Constitutional Court revised the elite compromise agreed after the Orange Revolution of 2004, restoring the old Ukrainian Constitution of 1996 and shifting the balance of power in favour of the president. The prosecution of Tymoshenko for 'abuse of office' began in May 2011. Wilson is right that this was a case of political persecution, when considered alongside other steps to monopolize power. But from a strictly legal perspective, it is questionable to brand Yanukovych an 'illegitimate' ruler. His actions were within the bounds of legal procedure, on the surface at any rate, and Tymoshenko was not innocent of the charges brought against her. The fact that her supporters called for the 'decriminalization' of the article under which Tymoshenko was sentenced was a tacit acknowledgement that she had indeed broken the law.

Yanukovych went on to monopolize political power for his own benefit and that of his 'Family' – in Wilson's telling, a Don Corleone–style clan of close relatives and confidants – while gradually pushing other oligarchs away from the trough. The author quotes a Ukrainian journalist explaining that the president 'wanted to be the richest man in Eastern Europe', and devotes many pages to corruption and extravagant lifestyles among the ruling clique. The sloppiness of his research is evident in his treatment of the alleged figures. In the space of three sentences, Wilson's estimate of the depredations of the Family soars from \$8–10 billion annually to \$100 billion overall, the latter figure attributed to post-Maidan Prime Minister Arseniy Yatsenyuk. Wilson doesn't bother to investigate the facts, but \$100 billion is surely a wild exaggeration. Total state revenues in 2014 were less than \$40 billion; if this figure were accurate, the departure of Yanukovych alone should have given a huge boost to the Ukrainian economy. The fact that exactly the opposite happened should have given Wilson cause to doubt Yatsenyuk's claim – and the idea that Yanukovych's corruption, though obviously present, was the greatest problem facing Ukraine.

In line with this approach, Wilson suggests that there was nothing problematic for Ukraine in the EU Association Agreement; the troubles lay with Yanukovych and Russia. *Ukraine Crisis* argues that Ukraine's Mafioso elite was simply too greedy: instead of embracing 'European values' and the salvation of the EU's structural reform, Kiev switched into 'bribery mode', trumping up claims about lost Russian trade. Wilson offers no serious discussion of the economic consequences the Association Agreement was (and is) likely to have for Ukraine. The either–or choice between a free-trade zone with the EU and a customs union with Russia jeopardized the remnants of Ukraine's high value-added industries, which were mostly connected to ex-Soviet manufacturing chains and stood little chance of surviving in direct competition with West European firms. In 2013, more than half of Ukrainian exports to the EU consisted of low value-added agricultural and metallurgical products, with just 13 per cent coming from the machine-engineering sector – against 30 per cent of exports to Russia and the other cis states. When these costs were taken together with the austerity measures accompanying International Monetary Fund (IMF) credit lines, the Ukrainian government had ample grounds for seeking to extract more concessions in return for signing the EU Agreement.

Although Wilson's analysis of contemporary Ukraine has involved detailed attention to its rival clans, he never asks whether Yanukovych's monopolization of power and 'rule-breaking' on the division of assets could have given some of the outmanoeuvred and frightened oligarchs a strong incentive to support and even radicalize the Maidan, in order to remove a serious threat to their own power, wealth and property. Of course, a serious answer to this question would require extensive research into the financial, infrastructural and media support for the protests, as well as thorough investigation of a number of suspicious episodes that involved seemingly irrational escalations of violence. This question is particularly vital in light of Maidan's political outcome – when, despite strong popular mobilization, anti-oligarchic rhetoric and a widespread distrust of the established opposition parties, there was no serious challenge to the top-down process of power reallocation after Yanukovych's flight.

In Wilson's characterization, Maidan was an Uprising with a capital U: a protest from below, with progressive demands and broad popular support across the country, legitimately defending itself against police repression; the 'Revolution of Dignity', as it is now almost officially called in Ukraine. In the introduction to his book, Wilson strains to slot Maidan into a larger 'cycle of global protest', associating it with the Occupy movement, the Spanish *indignados* and Egypt's Tahrir Square protests, though he is obliged to note its *differentia specifica* – reverting to a 'uniquely Ukrainian' and 'old-fashioned' world of projectile cobblestones, Molotov cocktails and violent confrontations with the police, in implicit contrast to the peaceful and carnivalesque 'Twitter revolutions'. Wilson does not ask why the Maidan supporters borrowed only tactics from the global Occupy wave, but were so radically different in their protest's framing and ideology. Why did Ukrainians wave EU flags when anti-austerity protesters inside the EU were more likely to be burning them – and without raising the banners of any exterior power?

Why did the Maidan activists not attempt to forge ties of solidarity with protest movements elsewhere? These contrasts and omissions suggest that Maidan was really a mobilization of a very different kind, one that bore only a superficial resemblance to global progressive movements: it had borrowed certain elements of their protest repertoire because it faced similar tactical problems and options in clashes with the police, but did not share – or at least, was not able to articulate – similar goals and grievances.[1] Wilson's attempt to force a fundamentally different form of mobilization into the same category as Occupy, the *indignados* and the Arab Spring is effectively a rhetorical move, aimed at bestowing a left-liberal legitimacy upon Maidan.

Ukraine Crisis's two chapters on Maidan are essentially a polemic against its Russian critics. They avoid any satisfactory discussion of the issues that might complicate Wilson's narrative: the significance of reactionary elements in the protest movement and the limits of its popular support. Thus, if all of Yanukovych's irrational, inconsistent and ultimately self-defeating repressive moves are explained by his evil desire to retain unchecked power, then violent escalations and ugly incidents on the protesters' side can easily be ascribed to government *agents provocateurs*, with no more evidence than a dubious online source or an anonymous interview. Wilson's discussion of Maidan's far-right current repeats the clichéd arguments that Maidan was a diverse and multi-ideological movement, in which activists from the ultra-nationalist Svoboda party and the Right Sector constituted a tiny minority. We are assured that the right wingers who did participate were not really 'fascists' in the strict sense of the term, so there is no need to be afraid of them; the fact that they were defeated in the 2014 elections proves that the 'fascist threat' was little more than a Russian propaganda myth. In any case, Wilson insists, the far right was covertly supported by Yanukovych himself, as a tame opposition, and had been used in 'provocations' against opposition protests before. There is very little corroborating evidence for this claim – Wilson's source is an article on a pro-Maidan website – though it is widely asserted by Ukrainian liberals; conveniently, it helps to downplay internal causes for the rise of the far right, including the responsibility of anti-communist liberals.

Wilson does not attempt to answer the obvious counter-arguments to his assertions about the far right. First, well-organized radical minorities can play a disproportionately significant role in protest movements, and Maidan offers a striking confirmation of this rule. Our work at the Kiev Centre for Social and Labour Research (CSLR) has shown that members of the far right were the most visible collective agents in the protests, above all during episodes of violence.[2] Second, the label attached to the Ukrainian far right – 'fascists' or 'national conservatives' – is less important than the need to combat its anti-democratic and xenophobic ideas and practices. Third, whether or not Yanukovych succeeded in exploiting the actions of the far right, it had its own agenda and would only have acquired more space to pursue it. Finally, electoral support is just one dimension of political influence. If members of the far right are now legitimated as heroes of the 'revolution' and the war – if they have secured top positions within the security apparatus and have been allowed to establish armed military units under their control – these are developments that cannot be downplayed or even justified, in the name of patriotism, as many in Ukraine are willing to do at present.

Discussion of the regional dimensions of the protests is astonishingly weak in *Ukraine Crisis*, which concentrates disproportionately on Kiev and devotes less than half a page to the maidans in other regions. Systematic research conducted by the CSLR's team has shown that only 14 per cent of Maidan protests took place in Kiev, with two-thirds occurring in the western and central regions. A more extended discussion of the regional aspect would have compelled Wilson to recognize that Maidan did not have majority support in the southern and eastern regions, which had predominantly voted for Yanukovych. The modest scale of many southeastern maidans was presumably one of the main reasons they were so easily repressed. Moreover, if Wilson had looked in more detail at the western maidans, he would have been obliged to qualify his claim that Maidan was not an 'armed revolution'.

By 20 February 2014, when Wilson describes 'barely armed' Maidan protesters in Kiev being shot by (still unidentified) snipers, Yanukovych had effectively lost control of the western regions, where his opponents had captured a large stock of weaponry from police and military sources – usually without facing serious resistance – and were bringing them to the capital. Wilson himself is told by Oleksandr Danylyuk, leader of the Common Cause NGO, that his men opened fire on the snipers, whose conversations they could intercept – Wilson doesn't ask how – using arms from 'various sources'.

In other words, Maidan was indeed an armed uprising, responding to sporadic government violence with a violence of its own, heavily skewed in terms of regional support, and with a significant far-right presence.[3] It drew strength from mass popular mobilization but failed to articulate social grievances, allowing itself to be represented politically by oligarchic opposition forces. Ultimately, it brought a neoliberal-nationalist government to power in Kiev. What sort of reaction was to be expected from the people of the southeastern regions, who had voted for Yanukovych and did not support the EU Agreement or the protests? These people were frightened by Maidan's violence and by the first moves of the Yatsenyuk government against the status of the Russian language. To be sure, such fears were exacerbated by Moscow's TV propaganda, but they had a real basis nonetheless. For Wilson, the answer is simple: they should simply have stayed at home and not protested at all. He effectively reduces the whole 'Eastern Imbroglio' – the heading of his chapter on events in eastern Ukraine – to Russian military intervention and oligarchic manipulation, presenting the Donbass region as a 'criminal Mordor' that has now spawned a revolt of 'lumpens against Ukraine'. Wilson's discussion of these crucial events relies on even shakier sources than his preceding chapters, often drawing on the accounts of Western and Ukrainian figures whose bias is patent. The whole section on Yanukovych's possible involvement in the Donbass uprising is based on information gleaned from an (unnamed) Ukrainian security officer, anonymous pro-Kiev 'Donbass activists' and the journalist Dmytro

Tymchuk, whose unreliability is well known. Of 117 endnotes in the central chapter about the war in the east, just two cite pro-Russian separatist sources.

A less prejudiced view – and one less reliant on lazy stereotypes about the culture of the Donbass – would recognize that the anti-Maidan movement in the east was the mirror image of the Maidans of the west. Both protests were driven by a mixture of just causes and irrational fears, and both were ultimately channelled into a confrontation between competing (and mutually reinforcing) imperialisms, Western and Russian, and nationalisms, Russian and Ukrainian. While Crimea undoubtedly saw a Russian special operation put into effect, it is wrong to suggest that all those who participated in decentralized anti-Maidans in Donetsk, Lugansk, Kharkov, Odessa and many other cities were mindless puppets of a similar project. Media and scholarly discussion alike have tended to focus excessively on cultural issues, paying much less attention to the economic basis of Ukrainian regionalism and the politics to which it gives rise. Differing attitudes towards the EU Agreement or the customs union with Russia, regionally differentiated geopolitical orientations and participation in Maidans or anti-Maidans are not simply the product of history and cultural identity: they are also rooted in conflicting material interests. Just as someone living in western Ukraine with relatives working in Spain, Poland or Italy might hope for deeper Euro-integration and the freedom to work without visas, their counterpart in the east with a job in heavy industry would have a stake in stable and peaceful relations with Russia. These divergent interests are not antagonistic: we are not speaking of class conflict in the true sense, but imperialist and nationalist competition may make them *appear* mutually exclusive.[4]

The hectic narrative of *Ukraine Crisis* is spattered with elementary mistakes. Wilson's errors in calculating the interval between Eastern Orthodox and Western Christmases (he has it as eleven days, not thirteen), or in deciphering the acronyms of nationalist guerrillas of the 1940s and '50s (the Ukrainian Insurgent Army or UPA becomes the 'Ukrainian People's Army') are surprising for an author who has been studying the

country for more than two decades. Another basic howler is more serious.
Wilson attempts to calculate how long Crimea belonged to Russia and
Ukraine respectively, concluding that it was part of Russia for just thirteen
years more and dismissing Russian claims for historical precedence on this
basis. The argument is strange enough on its own terms – when have such
calculations had any real political significance, other than to legitimate
dubious and contested territorial claims? – but is also based on a false
premise: that the Crimean Autonomous Soviet Socialist Republic was not
part of Russia before 1945. In fact, it was part of the Russian Soviet
Federative Socialist Republic, with a status clearly lower than that of the
Ukrainian, Belarusian and other Soviet Socialist Republics that were
formally equal to Russia and could themselves incorporate other
autonomous republics within their borders. This is an elementary fact for
anyone familiar with the structure of the USSR.

In some respects, the most revealing sections of *Ukraine Crisis* are those
on the international context. An insufficiently martial, 'postmodern' EU is in
large part to blame for the disaster. Following Robert Cooper, Wilson argues
that 'nineteenth-century shibboleths' like state sovereignty and hard power
have been largely replaced by smart interaction, non-state actors and shared
sovereignty – though he decides in the end that the EU is 'a mixture' of postmodern factors and old nation-state traditions, the latter reinforced by the
2008 financial crisis. Russia also mixes the traditional and the postmodern,
but in a different way. While travelling in the opposite direction – from
multinational union to traditional nation-state – Russia has 'leapfrogged'
into a postmodern political culture of ultra-cynical manipulation, where
'everything is permissible and there is no higher truth'. This makes the EU
particularly vulnerable, Wilson claims, as the fiendish new Russia inverts
Western 'soft power', deploying Western values against the West itself: culti-
vating its own fifth columns of pro-Russian NGOs, political parties and
other civil-society structures in neighbouring countries, fighting an
'information war' via TV and the internet, imitating mass mobilizations,

insisting on tolerance for diversity, and so on. Needless to say, Wilson does not attempt a systematic comparison between European or US soft power and the Russian alternative, although it would be safe to assume that covert Russian influence is largely confined to its neighbourhood, unlike Washington's global reach. *Ukraine Crisis* claims that Moscow's support for sympathetic parties, politicians and NGOs in Eastern Europe comes to $8 billion a year, which would be striking if true: by comparison, Victoria Nuland gave a figure of just $5 billion for US 'democracy promotion' efforts in Ukraine during the whole post-Soviet era. However, the only source for Wilson's estimate is a conversation with a Lithuanian defence minister.

Ukraine Crisis concludes with an attack on EU passivity. Brussels, Wilson had explained in an opening chapter, 'cannot cope with the big stuff like Russia or old-fashioned war at the edge of Europe'. Few EU member states are spending enough on weaponry; they have to be literally dragged into combat. Fortunately, NATO had taken charge of bombing Yugoslavia in the 1990s, 'saving Europe from its embarrassing inaction'. Germany is a poor excuse for an EU foreign-policy leader, since its post-war history rules out the use of military force. As the fighting in the Donbass rumbled on, with Kiev's 'anti-terrorist operation' combating Moscow's 'deniable intervention', Berlin was guilty of 'selective pacifism' in pressing Ukraine to 'lay down its arms'. Culpably, its first priority was that the fighting should stop, 'regardless of guilt'; it allowed Russia to negotiate from positions gained by subversion, rather than pressing for the status quo ante. Worse still, Ukraine may not be hurried into NATO as fast as Wilson would like. This is the context for Wilson's appeals to 'higher truths' and 'European values', to the defence of 'basic rights and freedoms we now take for granted in the West'. In tandem with passages demonizing the opposing power – Russia is predictably compared to Nazi Germany – and stigmatizing any opposition as 'useful idiots', Wilson's ideological boilerplate merely serves to legitimate imperialist interests and pro-war mobilization in a time of sharpened inter-state rivalry.

What of Ukraine's future? Wilson's best outcome is for Kiev to recover complete authority over the east. He has called for the EU to work 'vigorously and pro-actively' towards monitoring the Russian–Ukrainian border, and to escalate sanctions if Russia does not remove all military hardware from the separatist regions. As a second-best option, a frozen conflict might still allow Ukraine to 'move West', as he puts it; he can even contemplate Kiev cutting the Donbass loose, which might disconcert Moscow – though he quickly adds that the West would oppose it, as would many in Ukraine. Nevertheless, a smaller Ukraine might be 'more manageable', he writes in *Ukraine Crisis*. There could be grounds for hoping its famously 'overlapping or hybrid national identity' might be consolidated in a new 'political nation' which would know neither Jew nor Hellene. Totally dependent on the West for financial help, without ambitions for an independent foreign policy, this manageable Ukraine would then ideally implement radical neoliberal reforms in the style of Georgia's Saakashvili.

Regrettably, Wilson admits, the type of 'big bang' restructuring undergone by the Baltic states in the 1990s must be ruled out for the time being, but he dismisses the notion that 'economic reform would lead to social explosion' – this was 'the same old hack thinking that had held Ukraine back since 1991'. On the contrary, he suggests that the Poroshenko–Yatsenyuk government should see the eastern crisis as an opportunity to press ahead with sweeping changes in the rest of the country. The restraints on the new administration were largely political: after Maidan, 'much of the old regime remained intact', and 'the old oligarchy was at least temporarily stronger'. Wilson sighs over Yatsenyuk's decision to include the far-right Svoboda party in his government as 'a proxy for the moral authority of the radical forces on the Maidan'; but he is upbeat about the introduction of market prices for energy, and he cheers the passage of the EU Agreement. Under the policies he recommends, utility bills have doubled, inflation was running at 60 per cent in April 2015 and billion-dollar loans from the IMF are going straight to Kiev's creditors. Patriotic exhortations may not be enough to cushion the post-Maidan government from further discontent.

3

A Comedian in a Drama

25 April 2019

US readers won't be too surprised by a tale of an inexperienced candidate winning against the establishment's pick. But in the case of Ukraine's new leader, Volodymyr Zelenskyi, this widely made comparison is even something of an understatement. Imagine that Donald Trump was thirty years younger and had never written any books or participated in any (even allegedly) serious debates. There were no primaries and no GOP to take over. And Zelenskyi is a professional comedian.

But the comparisons with Trump have their limits. Zelenskyi, the son of a university professor and an engineer, is no working-class hero, but he is also no oligarch like outgoing president (and defeated second-round candidate) Petro Poroshenko, who made his fortune privatizing Soviet confectionery factories in the wild 1990s. The latter's aggressive nationalist campaign had far more in common with right-wing populists abroad, especially those in neighbouring countries, like Hungarian premier Viktor Orbán or de facto Polish leader Jarosław Kaczyński.

Poroshenko's main slogan was 'Army. Language. Faith.' and he raised the nationalist rallying cry 'Either me, or Putin.' In Sunday's second-round contest, a usually polarized society rallied in great numbers – 73 per cent

– against the incumbent. Zelenskyi won because he rode the wave of everything the unpopular incumbent symbolized, indeed for many kinds of voters. For them, Poroshenko meant poverty, unashamed corruption, the unending war in Donbass and aggressive nationalist initiatives in policies stretching from religion to language and public history. During pre-election debates at Ukraine's largest stadium, Zelenskyi literally called himself 'the result of your [Poroshenko's] mistakes'.

Yet the winning candidate had neither programme nor party, simply adopting the name of his TV show, *Servant of the People*. Zelenskyi arrives in office surrounded by 'new faces' who might not be the real decision-makers. Worryingly, he has murky relations with notorious oligarch Ihor Kolomoiskyi, who siphoned billions from Ukraine to offshore funds. As a politician, the new president-elect is uniquely shallow, and one can only imagine how poorly Ukrainians valued Poroshenko's 'achievements' and the developments of the five years since the Euromaidan uprising of 2014.

In this sense, the second round was a kind of referendum on Poroshenko but also the whole national-patriotic camp. The 'national-liberal' intelligentsia and a large part of pro-Western 'liberal' civil society aggressively rallied behind Poroshenko, attacking Zelenskyi and his voters as 'pro-Russian', unpatriotic, treacherous, dumb and uneducated. They said his victory would mark the end of Ukraine. Yet this Sunday we saw they represent barely a quarter of the country.

Five years after the Maidan uprising shook Ukraine, today we see that the political and intellectual establishment which came to power in 2014 has ended up in the same old bankruptcy. Indeed, the voters who elected Zelenskyi appear to be rather different from those whom enthusiastic Western media usually present as authentic representatives of Ukraine. Roughly speaking, we can say that his base doesn't like what the Russian government has been doing, but doesn't want to fight on to the bitter end either. They are probably pro-European but because of rather pragmatic reasons – the people to the west of Ukraine's borders live better than those to the east – and not because of the racist 'civilizational choice' (for Europe, against Russia) promoted by Ukrainian intellectuals.

They prefer to speak in Ukrainian, or in Russian, or in a mixture of both, but would laugh at the idea of making this into an ideological choice. They are tired of the confrontational atmosphere, the patriotic propaganda and constant search for 'Russian agents' under the bed. They are indifferent both to the Soviet Union and to the fanatical 'decommunization' of Soviet monuments and street names. They would rather be allowed to watch the banned Soviet movies, read Russian books and chat on Russian social networks without restrictions. They do not like pretentious patriotism and radical nationalism. They expect from the government tangible improvement of living standards for the majority, not the 'fight against corruption' for its own sake in the style of 'liberal' civil society.

Since the 2014 Euromaidan protests, the extreme pro-Russian segment of Ukrainian public life has been repressed and marginalized. Between 2014–19, an extreme pro-Western and nationalist current had instead become very prominent. Despite pro-democratic rhetoric, the forces thus raised to power had in fact shown remarkable authoritarian tendencies.

First was the case of banning the Communist Party of Ukraine. This was a major opposition party, indeed perhaps the largest in terms of real membership, supported by 13 per cent of voters in the 2012 parliamentary elections. Opposition politicians, media, journalists and bloggers suffered state repression and radical nationalist violence. This stretched as far as pogroms, arson attacks, imprisonment of opponents and fabricated criminal cases. So bad was the situation that the editor of the opposition's main online publication, Strana.ua, had to get political asylum in Austria. At the same time, a paid army of pro-Poroshenko trolls produced a toxic atmosphere intolerant of dissent. A number of university lecturers were fired or attacked for their political positions and forced to leave the country.

The conflict with Russia was a key to this atmosphere. In December 2018, after a likely deliberate provocation in the Kerch Strait ended in the arrest of Ukrainian ships and sailors by the Russian Navy, then-president Poroshenko pushed through martial law across half of Ukraine's regions. There was no evidence of an escalating threat from Russia; but this prospect was useful as a pretext for delaying elections and won some time for the beleaguered Poroshenko. According to polls, over 50 per cent of Ukrainians said they would never vote for him under any circumstances. Prolonging martial law and even repeating the provocation in Kerch Strait were seriously discussed among Poroshenko's entourage, but such schemes failed to receive support from Western leaders, most notably Angela Merkel.

Poroshenko would, at least, make the second round of the election when it was ultimately held: in the first round on 31 March he edged out former premier Yulia Tymoshenko thanks to vote-buying and even outright fraud in certain districts. However, both the US and EU were unwilling to let him force outright victory and an illegitimate re-election through such transparently deceitful methods, threatening to destabilize Ukraine. Local media reported that US diplomatic figures had assured Poroshenko that he would not be prosecuted after he had lost power.

Within Ukrainian ruling circles his influence was also waning. Powerful interior minister Arsen Avakov positioned himself as an independent guarantor of free and fair elections, while the far-right National Corps Party, with connections to Avakov, led a disruptive campaign against the corruption of Poroshenko's close business partners. Most other oligarchs seemed to oppose Poroshenko's re-election, as was evident from the reporting of political news by their TV channels.

Ultimately, the support for Zelenskyi was just overwhelming. Many observers tended to underestimate the scale of the opposition to the post-Maidan regime. Zelenskyi had a pro-EU and pro-NATO message, and even called a very divisive radical nationalist leader, Stepan Bandera, 'an undeniable hero'. Yet if in the traditionally anti-Western regions in the south and east of Ukraine, who usually think of Bandera as a Nazi collaborator, upwards of 80 per cent nonetheless voted for Zelenskyi, one can only imagine how much they wanted to get rid of Poroshenko. The margin of victory was nowhere near close enough for Poroshenko to have been able to attempt to rig the outcome.

In 2019 the peaceful transition of power, with Poroshenko's concession, was not a result of the strength of Ukrainian democracy but of Western dependency, oligarchic pluralism and the record-low support for the incumbent president in the second round. We still need to win democracy in Ukraine and, hopefully, Poroshenko's crushing defeat will open an opportunity for this.

As one leftist journalist commented, if you are not happy about Poroshenko's defeat, you have no heart; if you believe Zelenskyi's promises, you have no head. At this moment, when so many things are still unknown about Zelenskyi, most predictions about his policies are hardly more than reading the tea leaves. His personal views, exposed in a handful of interviews, are not a coherent ideology but just the libertarian dispositions of a successful showbiz figure who has not spent much time seriously thinking about political issues. Generally speaking, he is against excessive state interference in divisive issues regarding identity, the economy and private life, and favours a less confrontational approach to the war in Donbass and Russia.

He supports joining NATO and steps towards EU membership, but is also ready to communicate with and persuade those who oppose this. This is a break with those previously in power who despised (and had no problem alienating) this large minority in Ukrainian society. He is for some fiscal easing and, of course, like every politician in Eastern Europe, 'against corruption'. Zelenskyi has also spoken in favour of legalizing light drugs and sex work and against banning abortions, although these issues are on the periphery of political debates in Ukraine so far.

Yet it is still unknown how much his personal views are going to matter and how independent he will be as president. He was evidently supported by oligarch Ihor Kolomoiskyi and his popular TV channel, but the exact nature of the relationship and agreements between them is, perhaps, known to them alone. Kolomoiskyi may expect considerable compensation for the nationalization of PrivatBank – the largest bank in Ukraine, which he previously owned – but such a move would be very unpopular and would surely discredit the new president. We do not know how much influence his present advisors are going to have and who Zelenskyi will assign to the governmental offices.[1] At the same time, it is unknown who will form the core of Zelenskyi's party or, indeed, how he will relate to a parliament in which he has no faction of his own.

Nevertheless, there are certain structural constraints that any Ukrainian president would have to confront, limiting the possibilities for progressive politics in Ukraine. However, as yet, there are no serious grounds for the fears, expressed by some leftist observers, of a kind of neoliberal apocalypse under Zelenskyi. In fact, if there is anything certain about Zelenskyi's rule, it is that economic policy is going to be decided by the balance of the oligarchs' interests and IMF austerity requirements, just as it was under Poroshenko. Any radically alternative economic policy simply lacks any base in a significant political force.

Moreover, the rivalry between the oligarchs and the structure of Ukrainian civil society – where radical nationalists represent the strongest, best-organized and most-mobilized segment, while the liberals are weak and the left is almost non-existent – will surely put limits on any attempt to move beyond the national-patriotic consensus. Such moves will receive a strong street opposition from the nationalists, who are already whipping up fear about 'Russian revanchism'. And they may be supported by competing oligarchs – for example, if Poroshenko tries to consolidate national-patriotic opposition around him.

But the Ukrainian left does indeed now have a chance to become a stronger, more significant movement in the country's public life. Three undeniable results of Zelenskyi's victory benefit the left.[2] Firstly, the escalation of repression and nationalist trends in recent years have forced a weak and stigmatized left into a semi-underground situation. But Zelenskyi's victory promises the end of the mounting authoritarianism we saw under Poroshenko. Even if Ukraine's political regime remains structurally unchanged and we see another oligarchic group (for example, Kolomoiskyi's) attempting to monopolize power, there is at least a temporary moment of relief. Secondly, the hegemony of Ukrainian national-liberals who mostly consolidated around Poroshenko has been seriously challenged now. The crisis of their moral and intellectual leadership is already evident; more people see how irrelevant their vision of Ukraine and its future, which has been defied by the overwhelming majority, is. We are going to see many reflections about what has gone wrong, raising interest and opening opportunities for alternative political tendencies, including the left.

Finally, Zelenskyi's campaign brought into politics those groups who have never been interested in it or felt excluded since Maidan: primarily, young urban people in southeastern regions. Meanwhile, most of the comedian's voters do not expect much of him except for the fact he is not Poroshenko. Faced with the inevitable disappointment in his rule, it can at least be hoped that many will not just return to their private lives, but will search for other, non-electoral forms of politics that can achieve deeper change.

It would be a mistake to have illusions about Zelenskyi's promise of a 'new politics', or about breakthroughs in the campaign against corruption, peace in the Donbass or a reversal of the gains the far right has seen in recent years. All this will, without doubt, take much more than getting rid of Poroshenko alone. However, the first step has been made – and the weakening of the outgoing regime opens up more opportunities for the future.

4

From Ukraine with Comparisons: Preliminary Notes on Belarus

I began making these quick comparative notes the day after the first night of protests following the disputed 2020 elections in Belarus between Aliaksandar Lukashenka, who has ruled the country since 1994, and the opposition candidate Sviatlana Tsikhanouskaia. It is amazing how much was immediately predictable. In the absence of a radical vanguard, the initial spontaneous violence rapidly dissipated. Contrary to some political-science theories, the subsequent turn to large-scale non-violent opposition failed in the face of a consolidated ruling elite whose repression was unprecedented. The strike attempts were more wide-reaching than expected, but ultimately politically insignificant. Meanwhile, the pro-Lukashenka electorate remained overwhelmingly passive.

Belarusian society was polarized, in ways reminiscent of Euromaidan in Ukraine. Despite the appeals to 'national unity' and the avoidance of geopolitics in the rhetoric of protesters, all the typical pro-Western/pro-Russian cleavages were reproduced.[1]

When I wrote the notes, the extent of the Russian factor in Lukashenka's support and the place of Belarusian events in the escalating crisis of the post-Soviet world were less clear to me. Behind the dynamics in Belarus was precisely the same class conflict that is now being resolved with incomparably greater violence in Ukraine (on which see also Chapter 8, below). Belarus has become a much worse country to live in. Within a year and a half, Lukashenka would be allied with Putin, assisting in the full-scale invasion of Ukraine.

10 August 2020

1. Both Lukashenka and Tsikhanouskaia claim around 80 per cent of votes. The official results look suspicious, as they are improbably stable. Lukashenka gets around 80 per cent of votes in his fifth election in a row, despite all the ups and downs, particularly the COVID crisis? But the 70 to 80 per cent that Tsikhanouskaia claims may be even further from the real level of support. It is extremely hard to believe that a person who was virtually unknown just a few months ago could receive the overwhelming majority of votes in a tightly controlled election without the support of any popular media besides oppositional websites and Telegram channels. This is not a case of Volodymyr Zelenskyi, Donald Trump or Beppe Grillo, who, while political outsiders, were nevertheless also popular media stars before they became politicians.

An important Machiavellian lesson for other authoritarian leaders who do not disband elections completely: some regular credible independent polls are vital for maintaining rule, because otherwise the elections stop being a tool for political legitimacy, even if the leader in reality is not that unpopular. It's better to manipulate public opinion, as Putin does more or less successfully, rather than silence it completely, let the opposition claim a landslide victory in the vacuum of credible data and provoke an uprising that must then be dealt with violently.

2. Voters' real preferences are not that important now, as forces on the streets rule. But the protesters have problems with the use of efficient, strategic and coordinated violence. Actually, what we have seen at night in Belarus is what the Ukrainian Maidan radicalization could have been if it had indeed been just 'regular people' who 'spontaneously' turned to violence in response to government repression (as, unfortunately, too many

journalists, researchers and simply propagandists claimed in 2014 regarding, for example, the supposedly irrelevant role of the radical nationalists). In Belarus, and in Ukraine until recent years, the 'repertoire of contention' – widespread cultural expectations about the appropriate forms of political contention, including forms of protest – has not included violence. Two consecutive generations born after the 1950s saw large-scale protest violence only in TV broadcasts about events in other countries. They never experienced it directly in their countries, unlike citizens of Western democracies, where the *gilets jaunes* and George Floyd protests are rare events but not that extraordinary. So, when 'regular people' here turn to violence really spontaneously, these are chaotic, dispersed, uncoordinated clashes without the use of any tools of violence, and largely harmless for the riot police. On the other hand, when organized radical groups who have been training for their 'national revolution' for years are the drivers behind a violent escalation, they immediately bring Molotov cocktails, cobblestones, sticks. At later stages, they use firearms. They organize stable paramilitary units. They strategically take the loci of power in the capital and in the regions. One can read how this happened in Ukraine, and how exactly the radical nationalists were able to play such a key role in the Maidan radicalization, in my recently published article.[2]

But this scenario seems unlikely to be repeated in Belarus right now. The riot police have actually shown some signs of overextension at night. Concentrated in Minsk, they did not appear very efficient in the provincial cities. However, in order to take power in the regions, the opposition would need efficient nationwide structures that could coordinate assaults on regional offices by organized violent groups. It does not seem like Tsikhanouskaia's team has anything like this. There are not even loose opposition party structures like in Ukraine which, by the way, had majorities in many regional and city councils in 2014 that openly disobeyed Yanukovych.

3. Some are expressing hopes for political strikes. However, efficient non-violence does not happen spontaneously either. It requires its own

coordinating and mobilizing structures and resources. For efficient political strikes, for example, strong labour organizations are essential. As in other post-Soviet countries, Belarusian labour organizations are loyal to the government. The last large-scale strikes were in the 1990s. Independent labour is very weak. Moreover, in the case of Ukraine, the fact that the Maidan protests started non-violently and had a largely non-violent initial two-month-long phase was important for legitimating the turn to violence later on (and also for the attrition of the underfinanced police). In Belarus, violent clashes of an unprecedented scale started immediately. They won't attract Lukashenka supporters to the side of the protesters, and won't help to win over hesitating citizens or gain the sympathies of police officers. In contrast to its meaning for the cheerleaders of the Ukrainian 'Revolution of Dignity', 'Maidan' turned into a swear word for many people in Russia and Belarus, for whom it now means a violent political disaster. The very same people who claimed that 'Maidan is a spontaneous, peaceful, democratic protest' in 2014 need to claim now that 'this in Belarus is nothing like Maidan'. The violent clashes last night only increase the fears of those who valued Lukashenka's stability in contrast to the 'vibrant democracy' in Belarus's southern neighbour.

4. Some have noted that the police actions in Belarus do not really exceed the 'policing repertoire' of the Western democracies in relation to the *gilets jaunes* in France or the Black Lives Matter protests in the US. However, in the Belarusian context, where large-scale street violence has been absent in the past, the police actions were unprecedented. So was the use of police force during Maidan in Ukraine. However, unlike the Ukrainian oligarchy, who feared for their Western bank accounts and property, Lukashenka is ready to go until the very end in violent escalation, and he will likely not hesitate to order the use of the army where the riot police reach the limits of their capacity in dealing with provincial unrest.

Lukashenka cannot rely on anything except force. He is not like Maduro in Venezuela, who could withstand very strong pressure both inside the country and internationally. Unlike Maduro, Lukashenka cannot claim the legacy of a popular revolution; he does not have any party or movement to mobilize supporters. While Lukashenka's legitimacy has been based on restoring stability in the midst of the 1990s collapse, and preserving Soviet industry and some welfare, this is not enough to inspire enthusiastic support for his continuous rule.

5. Basically, this means that Lukashenka's rule now relies exclusively on the loyalty of the enforcement institutions. Unless it cracks, Lukashenka will withstand the inefficient violent and non-violent protests, which will fade away gradually. A split among the enforcers is most likely in the case that some generals get serious promises and guarantees from abroad. However, Russia and China have already recognized Lukashenka. It is not clear that the EU and US will go further than expressing 'deep concerns', or that there is a consensus among Western elites that they really need another point of conflict with Russia (and China).

6. In the case that Lukashenka withstands the protests, his regime is going to be even more repressive, even though he will be forced to think hard about how to pass power to a loyal successor. If he can't find the solution for this problem, he may well end up like Qaddafi. In the less likely event of an opposition victory, it is going to happen after considerable bloodshed. It will leave Belarus highly polarized. The very weak civil and political society of Belarus does not have any alternative ideas for national development except the Western-oriented neoliberalism in nationalistic colours that is even less popular in Belarus than in Ukraine. Either way, Belarus is likely to become a worse country to live in.

19 August 2020

1. We will probably never know how Belarusians voted on 9 August. Nobody doubts that the results of the elections were falsified, but nobody has proved that Lukashenka actually lost them either. Attempts to

extrapolate votes based on non-random samples of protocols from the precincts gave estimates ranging from around 30 per cent to 60 per cent for Tsikhanouskaia. It means that the available results, including the official results, do not allow us to establish the winner. However, Lukashenka won't go for any recount or revote because it would trigger defection from the regime. If he agrees to anything like this, it means that he has conceded defeat, like Yanukovych did as a result of the Ukrainian 'Orange Revolution' in 2004. So far, Lukashenka is unmovable; he allows only a distant possibility of new elections after changes to the Constitution and a weakening of the powers of the next president. This would give him time and allow him to secure some guarantees. However, protesters are united around the demand for his immediate resignation. The violent radicalization ended last week, but Lukashenka's intransigence increases the chances of another round.

2. As I predicted, decentralized, loosely coordinated violence by young people on the first nights after the elections failed, and has not developed into anything comparable to the armed uprising in Ukraine in 2014. For that, one needs not only outraged people but also stronger organizations with skills in violent strategy. In Belarus, the use of Molotov cocktails or any other tools of violence has been very rare, attempted barricades were very shaky and no paramilitary formations have emerged. The riot police were well prepared, and where they were outnumbered, it seems that some army units were deployed too. The reported number of injured police officers is lower than during Ukrainian Maidan by an order of magnitude, and the number of detained protesters in Belarus is also higher by an order of magnitude. The protesters could not occupy and barricade any specific space or establish even a small 'autonomous zone' that disrupted the state order to serve as a focal point for mobilizing activities.

The clashes appeared to be on the decline already on the third night. Then, in the middle of the week, protest activities shifted to a non-violent repertoire, with women in white clothes standing in chains with flowers and calling for an end to the violence. The marches and rallies were emphatically non-disruptive, usually not affecting the road traffic even when there were large crowds, and thus met with little repression. The rallies culminated on Sunday, in the largest numbers ever seen in post-Soviet Belarus. The reported interviews with participants point to the stolen elections, police violence, mass arrests and torture as the major motivations for people to go to the protests. It looks like the excessive police violence on the first night backlashed, as has happened in many other protest campaigns, and scaled up the mobilization of Lukashenka's opponents. However, it also does not look like the protesters were able to bridge the cleavage to attract a significant number of Lukashenka's supporters or hesitating citizens to their side.

3. The labour unrest in large and significant Belarusian factories has been a major development, and something truly unprecedented in the context of post-Soviet anti-government protests and revolutions, in which strikes by atomized workers have not played any significant role. In the case of the large Belarusian public sector, sustained strikes in the key state-owned enterprises could be a major blow to the government. It has already become an innovation in the political protest repertoire in this region that the government was not prepared to deal with (unlike the violence), and it probably contributed to the shift towards de-escalation last week.

However, the scale of labour unrest is still miles away from being a 'general strike'. Frankly, most of these activities do not even qualify as strikes in the strict sense. They have mostly been petitions, meetings with management, and rallies in the plant yards and at the gates. Sometimes large groups of workers joined the opposition rallies in an organized way. There are only confusing, contradictory reports that production has actually stopped, even if partially, and, if so, only in a few plants. It is possible that this labour unrest will grow in scale. However, it is not yet clear how sustained and truly disruptive it is going to be, if coordinated only by spontaneously emerging strike committees and the equally inexperienced middle-class and elite opposition, which is quite distant from the workers' lives. As expected, the official trade unions are pro-government, and have even mobilized people for pro-Lukashenka rallies. In principle, there are many ways to divide the workers and break the strikes. The crowdfunded money from businesspeople and the diaspora reported by the opposition Telegram channels and the solidarity committee are not even close to being able to support thousands of workers during a sufficiently long-lasting strike, and may only discredit the strikes if perceived as corrupt. Another issue of concern is the lack of any socioeconomic demands in most strike petitions, focused exclusively on the general political demands of the opposition. Given this, many workers who did not vote for Tsikhanouskaia are unlikely to feel ashamed about not joining the strikes. The workers enter Belarusian politics not as a class conscious of its distinct interests but as anti-Lukashenka citizens who just happened to be located at the strategic positions of economic production.

This still raises the question of why even such limited labour unrest has not happened in other post-Soviet revolutions, particularly during the Ukrainian Maidan. There, the opposition called for strikes from 'day zero'; however, what actually materialized during three months of campaigning were non-disruptive rallies organized by pro-opposition local authorities in the western regions or by some university administrations. One explanation could be that, unlike other post-Soviet leaders, Lukashenka preserved more of the Soviet industry and its specifics. Concentrated in mono-industrial towns or industrial neighbourhoods, the workers bring community problems with police violence to their workplaces and spontaneously discover the power that forces the management to start a dialogue with them. One should recall that the significant and disruptive Soviet workers' strikes during *perestroika* and immediately after failed to be repeated later, after the industrial collapse.

The decentralized and leaderless beginnings of the Belarusian protests may point to another part of the explanation. In Ukraine, the opposition party leaders – millionaires representing billionaires – as well as the middle-class, pro-Western NGO activists, were not exactly the people one would expect to inspire workers' strikes, especially because the remaining large Soviet industries were concentrated in the southeastern, predominantly pro-Russian regions. Last but not least – and this may explain why even western Ukrainian workers did not join the protests in an organized way – the Ukrainian opposition, it seems, bet at quite an early stage on the increasing pressure on Yanukovych from the West and a violent takeover of power that may not be an option for the Belarusian opposition.

4. The initially decentralized protest is in the process of developing structures. Various media, medical, solidarity initiatives and striking committees are emerging. Yet if anyone at all can claim leadership at this moment, it is still Tsikhanouskaia and her electoral team. This raises the question of how responsible they are for the evolving protests, and who is actually going to take power after Lukashenka and what their interests and ideas are. The aspirations of the rank and file are a bad predictor of the consequences of a protest. What is much more important is who will actually be able to compete for power at the potential new elections, and who will be able to push for 'real changes' after a change of government. In this context it is worrisome that Tsikhanouskaia's 'Coordination Council for the Transfer of Power' is formed mostly from the national-democratic intelligentsia, businessmen and activists of marginal opposition parties and NGOs with freaky neoliberal and nationalist programmes that look like a copy-and-paste of Ukraine's post-2014 development. Now the opposition is trying to distance themselves from the programme of the 'Reanimation package of reforms for Belarus' that has actually been supported by some of the NGOs and parties in the Council. Every revolution forms a demand for truly 'revolutionary' change, and the question of who will have enough authority and resources to fill in the blanks, and with what ideas, is important.

5. Despite some low-rank and low-scale defection among police officers, journalists of pro-government media and a few officials, there are no signs of top-level defection among the elite or the police/military. In other

revolutions, we often received evidence about disagreements 'behind the curtains' only weeks or even months later from the reports of investigative journalists. However, the less confrontational and 'dialogical' style of some local authorities and management in Belarus towards the opposition may reflect not a change of loyalty but a general de-escalation, a 'hot air' strategy that buys time for Lukashenka.

It is noteworthy that quite significant rallies are being mobilized in support of Lukashenka around the country. The participants of the pro-Lukashenka rallies look poorer and older on average than the participants of the opposition rallies. Even according to opposition journalists, the pro-government rally in Minsk gathered around thirty thousand people. It was smaller than the opposition rally the same day, and transportation to Minsk or other cities was organized by pro-governmental structures. However, the participants looked genuine and enthusiastic in their support for Lukashenka and voiced rational fears about loss of jobs, industry and stability, and about violence. This is in sharp contrast with the pro-Yanukovych rallies in Ukraine that, it appears, only strengthened the illusion of the Maidan protesters – that is, that every conscious citizen supports Maidan and those who do not are sell-outs, marginals and traitors. Lukashenka is intensively exploiting the patriotic rhetoric of a 'Motherland in danger', while the opposition still needs to find a way to speak about Belarusian identity and the nation and not to repeat unpopular national-democratic ideas and rhetoric.

6. Forecasts of a Russian invasion of Belarus to save Lukashenka, or alternatively suggestions that Moscow will accept any resolution of the crisis in Belarus safe in the knowledge that the country's economy is so dependent on Russia, are based on misleading comparisons with Ukraine and Armenia. Russia actually abstained from a full-scale invasion of southeastern Ukraine in 2014. The costs of annexing Crimea – a peninsula with a sympathetic population fearing the recent violent change of power in the capital – are incomparably less than those of occupying Belarus, a much

larger country where there are already large opposition rallies going on. Armenia, by contrast, is a tiny country squeezed between two more powerful and hostile states (Azerbaijan and Turkey) that block most of its borders. There was much more to Putin's tolerance of the Armenian revolution two years ago than the mere fact that the country had a Russia-dependent economy. The consequences of Ukraine (and other former Soviet republics) breaking economic links with Russia did not prevent the USSR's collapse, nor Ukraine's association with the EU. There is also the fact that increasingly frequent revolutions in Russia's neighbourhood in recent years provide a direct example and inspiration for the Russian opposition. It does not motivate Putin to accept just any result in Belarus.

On the other hand, the weakness of any national-identity split in Belarus, compared to Ukraine, makes it more difficult to legitimate support for repression. If in the case of Ukraine it was seen as legitimate for Russians to save 'our Russian-speaking population' from alien 'Banderovites' in the western regions, in Belarus the whole people is 'ours', not just a part of it. It is not very legitimate in the eyes of the Russian population to support a government that beats 'our' people. It means that Russian intervention is likely to be limited and covert, and if Lukashenka does eventually lose control, Russia will likely impose itself as a mediator to secure its interests in a negotiated compromise. A change of power in Belarus would actually be 'led' by Moscow so as not to be perceived as a loss for Putin. And for this, any serious candidate to replace Lukashenka will need to do more for Russia than just hide its geopolitical preferences in the way the opposition is doing now.

7. Specifically regarding references to Ukraine in the current discussions about Belarus: first, claims like 'this is Maidan' and 'this is nothing like Maidan' by the government or opposition supporters are of the same nature as typical legitimation/delegitimation claims such as 'this is a pogrom, not a revolution', 'we are partisans, not terrorists', 'we are not fascists, just patri-ots'. If our goal is not to play this game but rather to understand and

illuminate what is going on in Belarus, a careful comparison is necessary in the place of labelling. Second, comparison with Ukraine can not only help us to understand Belarus, but also the other way around. Now we can see better what a really 'spontaneous', 'all-national', 'leaderless' protest looks like, and it looks very different than the Ukrainian Maidan. Third, any person with a tendency to refer to Ukraine only in the context of radical nationalists, regional splits and geopolitical rivalry, and to add that there is 'nothing like this in Belarus', starts to look as if they finally came to appreciate the reporting about Maidan by RT (formerly Russia Today). There were many serious problems with Maidan – vagueness of claims, incapacity for institution-building, polarization of subaltern classes, civic exclusivity – that are very relevant for Belarus. It looks like the rosy enthusiasm about Belarus because 'there are workers' is of the same nature as the previous cynical scepticism about Ukraine because 'there were fascists'.

5

The Post-Soviet Vicious Circle[1]

with Oleg Zhuravlev

October 2021

Thirty years after the dissolution of the Soviet Union, Ukraine may give a unique perspective on the post-Soviet condition, which should be understood as an unresolved crisis in the fundamental relations of representation between political elites and social-group interests. In economics, Ukraine is perhaps the best candidate to be called the northernmost country of the Global South. From basic indicators such as GDP per capita to the most urgent ones such as COVID vaccination rates, Ukraine usually lags behind its Central and Eastern European neighbours. In politics, a kaleidoscope of short-lived governments, frequently rebranded but ideologically poorly distinguished political parties and patronal 'oligarchic' networks have been exploiting the weakening of state institutions. The latter are under intensifying pressure from a civil society that has remained 'narrow' in the sense of institutionalizing the public activity of no more than a small minority of Ukraine's citizens. In culture, unifying trends have proved shaky and short-lived. Internationally, Ukraine is stuck between the adverse Russia and the non-accepting EU and NATO.

This is the case despite three revolutions in the span of a single Ukrainian generation, in 1990, 2004 and 2014. The original prognosis for the post-Soviet countries was democratization and a return to the 'main road of civilization'. Ukraine was supposed to follow the path of its Eastern European neighbours and successfully integrate into Western institutions. As time passed, more critical perspectives gained prominence. Perhaps it was not a case of the post-Soviet countries following the path of EU-integrated Eastern Europe but rather the other way around, as Kaczyński's Poland and Orbán's Hungary joined the 'illiberal club' of Putin's Russia and Lukashenka's Belarus. In this view, Ukraine was just a weaker version of a 'competitive', 'electoral' or other hybrid form of authoritarian regime that has never been able to consolidate itself because of national-identity cleavages, oligarchic pluralism and other local peculiarities.

Some analysts have argued for the abandonment of generalizing views about the post-Soviet condition on the grounds that the countries in the geopolitical space between Estonia and Tajikistan have become too divergent. However, the difficulty of specifying the post-Soviet condition may be eased if we look at these dynamics without wearing teleological glasses. What if the post-Soviet countries have not been 'moving' anywhere at all, but rather stuck in a continuing crisis that started well before the Soviet collapse? The unresolved character of the crisis is then the defining characteristic of the post-Soviet condition.

Oleg Zhuravlev and I have analyzed the post-Soviet condition using Gramsci's approach to the concept of hegemonic crisis. Post-Soviet societies were born as a result of the collapse of a communist hegemony that had tried to connect the interests of the subaltern classes of the Russian Empire with a project of universal human emancipation. A crisis of hegemony 'consists precisely in the fact that the old is dying and the new cannot be born'.[2] No other hegemony replaced the communist one after it degraded in the Brezhnev years.

As the historical research on Stalinism and the Khrushchev era shows, communist ideology was not simply 'imposed' upon society. Instead, it was also constituted by ordinary people's discursive practices of subjectification that were possible precisely because of communism's hegemonic character.[3]

A dense network of institutions mobilized the active consent of the broad mass of Soviet citizens under the political, intellectual and moral leadership of a Communist Party that oversaw the rapid modernization of Soviet society and victory over the existential threat of Nazism in World War II. Precisely because they were not solely tools of 'totalitarian' control, these institutions could serve as crucial infrastructure for massive civic activization during the partial liberalization under Khrushchev. Soviet citizens mobilized and articulated their grievances in the language of communist ideology, addressing the gaps between the party's hegemonic claims and the Soviet reality.[4] However, the Communist Party failed to integrate this wave of civic activization to rejuvenate, adapt and strengthen their hegemony; instead, the Thaw was aborted by a conservative reaction. The institutions of communist hegemony ossified into bureaucratic career ladders and political participation became increasingly formalistic and ritualistic.

Those authors who have applied Gramsci to post-Soviet societies have usually relied on the concept of 'passive revolution', a shorthand modelled on conservative Piedmont's leading role in the nineteenth-century Italian Risorgimento.[5] The concept has been applied to many different processes in various countries and time periods, becoming something of a 'portmanteau' term.[6] But there are crucial differences between the post-Soviet case and classical instances of passive revolution. For one thing, capitalist transformation in the ex-USSR was not a modernizing process but rather an 'involution' which undid some of the Soviet Union's major achievements. Triggered by Gorbachev in a failed attempt to revive state socialism from above, it ended in a centrifugal 'stealing [of] the state' by former members of the Soviet elite. The upshot of the USSR's disintegration was a weakening of state institutions, relegation to the periphery of the world economy and a series of de-modernization processes in society and culture.[7]

Post-Soviet elite formation took place in the context of economic recession and an extraordinarily rapid and arbitrary privatization of state property. As a result, across post-Soviet societies, the new elites lacked any source of popular legitimacy – they are still widely perceived as thieves and corrupt. We could describe this new elite as 'political capitalists', a fraction of the broader capitalist class whose major competitive advantage is access to selective benefits from the state – for example, informal relationships with government officials and often deliberately designed legal loopholes for tax evasion and capital flight that also facilitated hostile company takeovers from competitors. The severity of the post-Soviet crisis of hegemony manifested itself in low levels of trust in government, parties and official ideologies, narrow civil societies, and relatively frequent protest mobilizations. In most post-Soviet states that did not join the EU, patronal authoritarian figures like Putin and Lukashenka have peddled a narrative of stability as their main source of mass legitimacy. They rule through the passive consent of electoral majorities, patrimonial networks, tactical alliances, and coercion of the opposition. However, because the intermediate stratum between leader and masses remains weak, these regimes can become vulnerable to opposition uprisings and elite defection.

In a minority of post-Soviet countries (Ukraine, Moldova, Armenia, Georgia and Kyrgyzstan), the consolidation of 'Caesarist' rule has so far failed. For example, in Ukraine, among the six post-Soviet presidents, only one (Leonid Kuchma in 1999) was re-elected for a second term. In these countries, massive popular mobilizations with revolutionary aspirations have occasioned transfers of power. Three revolutions have happened in Kyrgyzstan over the last fifteen years. There were revolutions in Georgia in 2003 and in Armenia in 2018, while protests led to changes of government in Moldova in 2009 and 2015. Similar mobilizations with revolutionary aspirations have developed several times in Russia and Belarus, although they were ultimately unsuccessful in ousting the incumbents. Meanwhile, Ukraine has witnessed the 'Revolution on Granite' in 1990, the 'Orange Revolution' in 2004 and the Euromaidan or 'Revolution of Dignity' in 2014.

These revolutions have been remarkably consistent in failing to establish a more stable political order. Post-revolutionary leaders and parties have either quickly lost power or had significant problems with re-election. Institutional and structural changes have remained limited. It has become typical in these countries to view these revolutions as just another round of elite rotation that 'changed nothing'. How can we explain this pattern of frequent but deficient revolutions?

We argue that *maidan* revolutions have been deficient solutions to very real problems of political representation.[8] They combine revolutionary aspirations and repertoires of collective action with vaguely articulated agendas, loose structures of mobilization and weak and dispersed leadership. They generate a symbolic resource of revolutionary legitimacy for which political agents may compete and which they can hijack; however, they do not establish durable institutions. We illustrate this argument with the case of Ukraine's Euromaidan uprising – the most long-lasting, large-scale and violent revolution in the post-Soviet region.

Ukraine used to be notorious for its regional political polarization, attributed to either ethnolinguistic factors, divergent political cultures or a split in national identity and conflicting interpretations of what Ukraine should be among Ukrainians themselves. After all, the territories of present-day Ukraine were unified under a modern state only during World War II, after having been controlled by competing empires for centuries. Many claimed that the 2014 Euromaidan overcame these political fractures, finally uniting Ukraine's regions and ethnolinguistic groups in an inclusive civic nation. However, as we have demonstrated elsewhere, Euromaidan civic nationalism was of a specific, 'eventful' kind.[9] Euromaidan activists proclaimed national unity 'by default', hailing the participation of people from various parts of the country (even if the latter did not necessarily represent majority opinion in the southern and eastern regions). As a result, Euromaidan excluded those who remained sceptical about the protests and began to reproduce and intensify the very divisions that undermined nationwide political representation.

An upsurge in volunteerism after 2014 remained largely informal and did not go much further than supporting Ukrainian military efforts in

Donbass. Membership of civil-society organizations hardly increased.[10] What did change because of Euromaidan was the volume of resources available to a narrow civil-society wedge to intensify its pressure on the state. The protests strengthened the (neo)liberal and nationalist organizations that were claiming to speak on behalf of 'Ukrainian civil society' and by extension the nation as a whole.

The Euromaidan protesters distrusted political parties. Their response to 'dirty' oligarchic politics was the 'authentic' politics of civic mobilization and solidarity, which was not institutionalized into an autonomous political force. The formula of many regular protesters was the following: we are not engaging in 'dirty' politics; if the post-revolutionary government does not fulfil our expectations, we will organize another revolution against it.

None of the successful *maidans* has ever posed a threat of systematic expropriation to the post-Soviet ruling class of political capitalists. Even though *maidans* have articulated grievances against the ruling class in general ('oligarchs', 'cronies', 'mafia', etc.), they always left open to the majority of the ruling class the option of opportunistic maneuvering by joining the new governing bloc and comprador accommodation with the West. The overall result of *maidan* revolutions has been a shift in the balance of power between competing 'oligarchic clans' rather than their overthrow.[11] In Ukraine, the political benefits of Euromaidan were appropriated by Petro Poroshenko and other oligarchic politicians and parties who competed for the resource of civic legitimacy that the Euromaidan generated. At the same time, the Euromaidan amplified a demand for political representation that could not be met by 'politics as usual'. This is why Poroshenko lost his bid for re-election in 2019, even though he was cheerleading reforms that were aligned with Euromaidan nationalism. Poroshenko fell into a trap between inflated, poorly articulated and poorly organized mass expectations about post-revolutionary social progress and the well-articulated neoliberal and nationalist agendas of an empowered but narrow civil society allied with transnational capital.

Zelenskyi's landslide electoral victory in 2019 was a perfect symptom of the intensifying crisis of political representation. He succeeded not because of the attractiveness of a 'new face' but because of the 'extreme weakness' of the old politicians and parties.[12] A Gallup poll at the end of Poroshenko's rule recorded the lowest level of trust towards government institutions of any polled electorate in the world. The 2019 election brought together those disappointed with the lack of revolutionary change after the Euromaidan with those alienated by divisive nationalism. Zelenskyi's staggering level of support (73 per cent) cut across Ukraine's political cleavages much more than the Euromaidan had.

However, lacking any real party or populist movement, or even a coherent team or clear plan, Zelenskyi quickly fell into the same trap as Poroshenko, squeezed between the most powerful interests in Ukrainian politics (various fractions of political capitalists), the Western powers and civil society. Zelenskyi's non-divisive national rhetoric lacked policy ballast. The new president has neither accelerated nor revised the nationalist policies of Poroshenko and has been trying to compensate for the rising gap between inflated expectations and outcomes with selective prosecutions of oligarchs, opposition media and political parties. His contradictory manoeuvrings appear to be further intensifying the underlying crisis of hegemony.

The *maidan* revolutions purportedly aimed at fundamental transformation of the ruling order 'from below'. Falling short of this goal, however, they have become locked in a repetitive cycle that leaves the original problem unresolved. Is there a way out of this impasse? In Ukraine, the diminished autonomy of the state makes the country's political capitalists more vulnerable to being outcompeted and marginalized by transnational capital – reflected in their vehement resistance to 'anti-corruption'. This existential threat – far greater than any of the previous *maidan*s had ever posed – may force the post-Soviet ruling class to engage in more active attempts to unite, articulate and pursue their own interests and those of the subaltern classes. In their own turn, more successful hegemonic politics from above could give a model and open opportunities for counter-hegemony from below.[13]

2022

6

Three Scenarios for the Ukraine–Russia Crisis

16 February 2022

In late January, as Western countries escalated their rhetoric about an 'imminent invasion' by Russia, Ukrainian President Volodymyr Zelenskyi questioned this narrative at a press conference with foreign reporters. 'I'm the president of Ukraine and I'm based here and I think I know the details better here', he said following his phone call with US President Joe Biden. I felt proud and I think many other Ukrainians did, too.[1] In the 2019 presidential elections, 73 per cent of voters supported Zelenskyi, a comedian with no political experience, in an act of total rejection of the dinosaur of Ukrainian oligarchic politics, Petro Poroshenko, who ran on an aggressive nationalist platform. Despite his campaign promises to unite the nation and bring radical change to the country, Zelenskyi has largely veered away from this path. So, when he stood up to Western pressure, it was a rare moment of defiance in which he appeared close to the fictional teacher-turned-president Vasyl Holoborodko, who he portrayed in the popular TV show *Servant of the People*.

In the past two weeks, Zelenskyi has continued to call for calm, and he reassured Ukrainian citizens that his government has the situation under control. He announced a day of national unity on 16 February and called on

MPs and oligarchs who left the country to come back and show their support for the Ukrainian nation. But faced with warmongering narratives and panic, which are damaging the Ukrainian economy, the Ukrainian president has to go beyond mustering independent rhetoric. He needs to undertake proactive foreign policy in the interests of all Ukrainian citizens that would take seriously the critical issues behind the escalation. Ignoring them or unequivocally rejecting them on dubious grounds could deprive Ukraine of a say in its own future as decisions are taken on its behalf by foreign powers.

So far, the Ukrainian diplomatic initiatives have been rather short-sighted. It may seem smart to exploit the scare of the 'imminent invasion' to get more weapons from the West or campaign for preventive sanctions against Russia. However, the weapons that are currently supplied to Ukraine would not save it in case of an all-out attack by Russia. Similarly, the proposed sanctions by the West are unlikely to be consolidated or hurt Russia enough. The 'alliance' with the UK and Poland announced on 1 February is more of a publicity stunt by British Prime Minister Boris Johnson, who is in deep domestic trouble, than an effective pact that could guarantee protection for Ukraine. Not only does it not contain any viable commitments from London and Warsaw, but it is also a doubtful achievement for Ukraine to join the toxic company of some of the most right-wing governments in Europe.

The prospects of NATO membership also seem rather dim, despite the fact that Western powers have rejected Russian demands to make it official. At this time, the door seems to be closed, and continuing to knock on it may not be in the best interest of the nation. As Zelenskyi himself once said about NATO membership, 'I never go visiting unless I am invited. I don't want to feel inferior, a second-class person.' One of the apparent Russian achievements of the past year of escalation is that the issue of Ukraine's NATO membership has turned even more toxic and divisive. There is now even more concern as to whether accepting Ukraine would make all other NATO countries less secure as a result. It is also increasingly clear that a

Putin successor, however progressive or democratic they may be, would still see Ukraine's NATO membership as a threat.

This leaves us with three basic scenarios in the long term. The first one is a humiliating defeat for Russia and its loss of Great Power status in Eurasia. This is a hope held by the Ukrainian nationalist movement. Its members see Ukraine not only struggling for its sovereignty but also being part of dismantling the Russian Empire – a process that has been going on for over a century. They hope to see Chechnya-style conflicts erupt across the Russian Federation. The problem is that Ukrainian nationalists do not care what most Ukrainians would think about sacrificing themselves in a long-term crusade to turn Russia into a patchwork of small states. They also do not take into account whether the rest of humanity would really like to witness state collapse and civil war on the territory of a nuclear power.

The second scenario is an international agreement about Ukrainian neutrality or the so-called 'Finlandization' of Ukraine, which refers to Finland's historic decision to associate with Europe, but avoid hostility towards Russia by not joining NATO. The problem with this proposal is that it is unenforceable given domestic opposition to it, and there is little international faith that the Kremlin would commit to Ukraine's neutral but sovereign status. Ukraine needs stronger guarantees than a treaty that can be broken by Russia at any moment.

This leaves us with the third scenario, which would entail constructing an overarching security structure for the whole of Europe that would include both Ukraine and Russia.[2] This could start with regular regional security consultations, building new norms of behaviour between major powers, their allies, and non-aligned states, and developing detailed multilateral security guarantees re-affirmed by extensive military restraint and transparency confidence-building measures. The details of such a structure have already been laid out in a comprehensive proposal recently put forward by a large group of non-governmental experts from the US, EU, Russia and five countries squeezed between Russia and NATO, including Ukraine.[3] Such an arrangement could establish common security and economic space from Lisbon (or even Vancouver) to Vladivostok, as some hoped at the end of the Cold War. It is in Ukraine's vital interest to be among the initiators and active participants of this process and to shape its outcomes.

Restoring Ukraine's non-alignment status would be a necessary first step, which would require amending the Ukrainian Constitution. In 2019, amid Poroshenko's desperate attempts to get re-elected, the goal of 'Euro-Atlantic integration' was inscribed into the Constitution. While this constitutional change was legal, it was hardly legitimate, as Ukrainians were rather split on NATO at that time (see Chapter 7, below) and the parties that pushed for it were polling dismally in terms of public support.

No less importantly, Ukraine also needs a more constructive approach towards the Minsk Accords, whose implementation has been stagnating for seven years, although they follow the basic logic of all the major peace settlements of the last decades. This would require direct negotiations with the representatives of the separatist regions in the Donbass, which would be legitimated in elections. It would also require that Kiev changes its 'first border, then elections' approach, in which it demands that full control be regained over the Ukrainian borders before recognising any elections in the breakaway regions. Both Russia and the Russian-backed separatists are rejecting this sequence of events because they think it would allow Ukraine to re-impose its authority by force, which would lead to discrimination, repression and expulsion of hundreds of thousands of Ukrainian citizens perceived to be 'collaborationists'. In a recent interview, Oleksii Danilov, the secretary of Ukraine's National Security and Defense Council, claimed that the Accords are not possible to implement because Ukrainian society may not accept them, and Russia may exploit a 'very difficult internal situation' that may lead to the 'country's destruction'. Indeed, thanks to the deliberate delay in implementing the Accords, they are not as popular today as they were in 2015. Nevertheless, the majority of Ukrainians still believe that compromises will have to be made to achieve peace.[4]

One of the main reasons for the lack of progress with the Minsk Accords is not only fear among Ukrainian politicians of nationalist violence but also the change in electoral geography that would take place once the millions of Ukrainians isolated in breakaway regions rejoin the national electorate. They are unlikely to support either Zelenskyi or the nationalist opposition. There are also fears that, if a special status is accorded to these regions, this would give them veto power at the executive level and make Ukraine ungovernable. However, that is not the case. The only leverage the re-integrated areas would get is via the threat of an organised secession from Ukraine.

One of the solutions could be extending the special status to the whole territory of the Donbass rather than just the territories under separatist control, which was suggested by Enrique Menendez, a Ukrainian civic and humanitarian activist from Donetsk.[5] This may look like an unjustified concession to Russia and may provoke outrage among some Ukrainians. However, such a move would actually dilute pro-Russian sentiments, as people loyal to Ukraine would also be part of voting and decision-making in the local administration and would make secession much more difficult.

The Ukrainian political leadership should stop allowing itself to be blackmailed with threats of a nationalist revolt. After all, these threats are not about the Minsk Accords per se, but about any compromise with Russia that would cross the numerous red lines of the nationalist segments of Ukraine's political elite and civil society. Implementing the Minsk Accords means the capitulation not of Ukraine but of an unfeasible nation-building project in Ukraine driven by a vocal nationalist minority. It is a project that envisions the exclusion of Ukrainian citizens who would like to retain their native Russian language in the public sphere, embrace the achievements and history of Soviet Ukraine, and prefer friendly relations with Russia.

Implementing the Minsk Accords means recognition and institutional protection of the political diversity among Ukrainians, many of whom do not agree with the 'civilisational choices' made for them by that active minority since 2014.

The Ukrainian leadership should ask for support from its Western allies to work towards a national consensus on the Minsk Accords. A consolidated Western position would discourage the nationalist segment of civil society, which is dependent on the West for funding, from supporting any disruptive action against such an initiative. Kiev would also need to change the dominant discourse about the war in Donbass and start revising discriminatory and anti-democratic policies, particularly those related to language and history. It should also call for international aid, loans and investments to help rebuild and reintegrate the Donbass region, boost economic development and improve social provision across the country.

Whether Zelenskyi would be able to lead such efforts to resolve the current crisis is under question. Having no real party, no popular movement and not even a coherent team behind him, he has failed to reverse the nationalist-radicalization trends of Poroshenko's government and even escalated some of them. There is still time for Zelenskyi to change his strategy.[6] What would strengthen his power is reaching sustainable peace and solving the country's most pressing political problems that only divert scarce resources from socioeconomic development. He can still go back to his campaign promises for truly inclusive national unity and the image he carefully constructed around his fictional character that got him elected with such overwhelming support.

20 March 2022

The world is entering a major political and economic crisis as a result of the Russia–Ukraine war. Any outcome of the war will lead to economic, political and ideological transformations in the post-Soviet space. We can already observe how narratives appealing to the 'brotherly' Slavic people or memories of victory in World War II – which have outlived the Soviet collapse by more than thirty years and had wide appeal even in Ukraine, despite post-Euromaidan 'decommunization' policies – are now weakening. In the event that the military resistance in Ukraine and the crippling sanctions on Russia lead to the latter's defeat, such a humiliation would accelerate the collapse of Putin's regime. Whether via a *maidan* revolution or, more probably, a palace coup by a faction of the Russian elite, the upshot would be the ultimate failure of a sovereign centre of capital accumulation in the post-Soviet space. Elites in a weakened Russia and other post-Soviet states would reorient towards either the West or China, and would be forced to abandon their competitive advantages in the selective allocations of the state (aka 'corruption').

Removing the Russian sovereigntist pole in the post-Soviet space would reorganize regional politics completely, along with the structure of political alliances in the respective Great Powers. While the US, EU and China would also be re-ideologizing, as the New Cold War between them hardens, the counter-hegemonic responses from post-Soviet societies to their new hegemons might not necessarily be progressive. The longer the war goes on, and the more casualties and destruction that Russia's invasion is able to inflict, the greater the chance that Ukrainian state and military institutions will be weakened, which would then strengthen the appeal of radical forces – similar to what happened recently in the Middle East.

If Russia finds a way to withstand the economic blow of intensifying sanctions and internal political destabilisation, it would not be able to rely on escalating dictatorial measures and sheer repression indefinitely. The Russian state would need to buy the loyalty of Russians and subjugated nations through less fiscally conservative and more Keynesian economic policies.[7] The ruling elite would need to explain to society what so many Russian soldiers died for, what they killed so many of their Ukrainian 'brothers' for, what the people have been suffering sanctions for. Instead of the empty rhetoric of 'denazification' which has clearly been insufficient to inspire enthusiasm for the war, this would require a more coherent imperialist-conservative project connecting the interests of the Russian elites to the interests of subaltern classes and nations. It would also require stronger political institutions to mobilize active consent for a Russian hegemonic project – a ruling party with massive membership and a popular pro-governmental movement, or their equivalents in the digital age. At the same time, the unavoidable gap between the Russian elite's hegemonic claims and its actual policies would open an opportunity for a stronger counter-hegemonic project that would address this disparity. It is possible that once again the weakest link in the imperialist chain may offer the world a new model: a socially transformative revolution for the twenty-first century.

One way or another, then, the war may put an end to the post-Soviet condition, transforming or dismantling the geopolitical space formerly occupied by the USSR. The elites who amassed their fortunes in the process of rapid and arbitrary privatization of state property in the 1990s have struggled to secure broader legitimacy for their rule. Authoritarian leaders like Putin rose to power by serving an important function for this political capitalist ruling class, protecting their assets and opportunities for rent-seeking, stopping the self-damaging centrifugal processes of elite fragmentation and providing some popular legitimacy by restoring stability amid the Soviet Union's chaotic collapse. The source of that legitimacy did not include any kind of developmental project to lead the way out from the huge grey zone of stagnation and degradation. The post-Soviet crisis was prolonged rather than resolved.

The seemingly 'consolidated' authoritarian regimes in Belarus and Kazakhstan would likely not have been able to survive the recent massive protests without Russia's help. Russia's invasion of Ukraine is ultimately a way to compensate with brutal violence for the fact that the post-Soviet ruling elites have not acquired any power of attraction. Instead, a fraction of this elite consolidated around Putin acquired strong Great Power aspirations. At the same time, the abundant problems the Russian Army encountered in the first weeks of the war reveal the weakness of 'authoritarian modernization'. The economic consequences of the war for Russia undermine the very source of Putin's legitimacy: his promise to prevent the country from sliding into a disaster.

21 March 2022

Over the weekend, President Volodymyr Zelenskyi's government suspended eleven Ukrainian political parties, citing their alleged 'links with Russia'. While the majority of the suspended parties were small, and some were outright insignificant, one of them, the Opposition Platform for Life, came second in the recent elections and currently holds 44 seats in the 450-seat Ukrainian Parliament.

It is true that these parties are perceived as 'pro-Russian' by many in Ukraine. But it is important to understand what 'pro-Russian' means in the country today. Before 2014, there was a large camp in Ukrainian politics calling for closer integration with Russia-led international institutions rather than with those in the Euro-Atlantic sphere, or even for Ukraine entering into a Union State with Russia and Belarus. After the Euromaidan revolution, and Russia's hostile actions in Crimea and Donbass, however, the pro-Russian camp was marginalized in Ukrainian politics. And at the same time, the pro-Russian label became very inflated. It started to be used to describe anyone calling for Ukraine's neutrality. It has also started to be employed to discredit and silence sovereigntist, state-developmentalist, anti-Western, illiberal, populist, left-wing and many other discourses. This wide variety of views and positions could be grouped together and condemned under one label primarily because they all criticized and raised questions about pro-Western, neoliberal and nationalist discourses, which have dominated Ukraine's political sphere since 2014, but do not really reflect the political diversity of Ukrainian society.

But the parties and politicians who have been branded as 'pro-Russian' in Ukraine – and recently been suspended by Zelenskyi's government – have very different relations with Russia. While some may have links to Russian soft power efforts – though these links are rarely properly investigated and proved – others are actually themselves under Russian sanctions. Most 'pro-Russian' parties in Ukraine are first and foremost 'pro-themselves' and have autonomous interests and sources of income in Ukraine. They are trying to capitalize on the real grievances of a sizeable minority of Russian-speaking Ukrainian citizens concentrated in the southeastern regions. These parties do command significant public support. For example, three of the recently suspended parties participated in the parliamentary elections in 2019 and, combined, received about 2.7 million votes (18.3 per cent), and in the most recent polls conducted before Russia's invasion these parties collectively scored about 16–20 per cent of the vote.

Other parties on Zelenskyi's suspension list were of left-wing orientation. Some of them, such as the Socialist and Progressive Socialist parties, played an important role in Ukrainian politics in the 1990s and 2000s, but by now they are all completely marginalized. Indeed, there is no political party in Ukraine today with 'left' or 'socialist' in its name that could secure any considerable portion of the general vote now or for the foreseeable future. Ukraine had already suspended in 2015 all of the country's communist parties under the 'decommunization' law, which was strongly criticized by the Council of Europe's Venice Commission.

The latest round of suspensions may not necessarily be motivated by the wish to erase the left from Ukraine's political sphere, but it certainly contributes to such an agenda.

The irony is that the suspension of these parties is completely meaningless for Ukraine's security. It is true that some of the suspended parties, like the 'progressive socialists', were strongly and genuinely pro-Russian for many years. However, practically every leader and sponsor of these parties with any real influence in Ukraine condemned Russia's invasion, and such people are now contributing to Ukraine's defence.

Moreover, it is not clear how the suspension of party activities would help to prevent any actions being taken by members or leaders of these parties against the Ukrainian state. The Ukrainian party organizations are typically very weak as political or activist collectives, perhaps with the partial exception, among the suspended parties, of the Party of Sharii, founded by one of Ukraine's most popular political bloggers and now focusing on humanitarian activities. Those who are thinking about collaborating with Russia, either directly with the Kremlin or through its propaganda network, amid the invasion would do this outside of party structures. They would have no reason to try and move Russian money via their party's official accounts.

All this signals that the Ukrainian government's decision to suspend left-wing and opposition parties has little to do with any objective wartime security needs of Ukraine, and much to do with the post-Euromaidan polarization of Ukrainian politics and redefinition of the Ukrainian identity that pushed a variety of the dissenting positions beyond the borders of tolerable discourse in the country. It also has to do with Zelenskyi's attempts to consolidate political power, which began long before the Russian invasion.

Indeed, the decision to suspend the parties follows a pattern. Since last year, the government has imposed sanctions on opposition media and some opposition leaders on a regular basis, without providing any convincing evidence of wrongdoing to the public. One year ago, for example, the government sanctioned Viktor Medvedchuk, a personal friend of Putin, soon after polls started to show that his party may have more public support than Zelenskyi's Servant of the People Party and could overtake him in a future election. At the time, the sanctions against Medvedchuk and his TV stations were also endorsed by the US Embassy in Ukraine. Several analysts have since speculated that those sanctions may have been among the factors that led Putin to begin preparations for the war, by convincing him that Russia-friendly politicians would never be allowed to win an election in Ukraine.

Now, Medvedchuk has escaped house arrest and is hiding from Ukrainian authorities. The Opposition Platform for Life removed him from the party leadership, condemned Russia's invasion and called its members to join the forces defending Ukraine.

While it is easy to classify the decision to suspend the 'pro-Russian' political parties amid a Russian invasion as a security necessity, the move should be analyzed and understood in this wider context. It is also important to point out that the government's sanctions regime against opposition parties, politicians and media has long attracted widespread criticism within Ukraine. Many in the country believe that the sanctions were designed and implemented by a small group attending Ukraine's National Security and Defense Council meetings, without serious discussion, on dubious legal grounds, to further corrupt interests.[8]

This is why there is little reason to expect the suspension of the parties to be lifted once the war is over. The Ministry of Justice will likely take legal action and ban the parties permanently.[9] This, however, will help neither the war effort nor the political ambitions of the current government. In fact, they could push some Ukrainians to collaborate with Russia.

Indeed, so far collaboration with the invaders in the occupied areas has been minimal. There is no indication that the public will get behind a pro-Russia party or politician in large numbers. And while Russia would certainly approach these parties first if it decides to install a puppet government in Ukraine, many in their political cadres would likely decline the offer – they would not want to risk their capital, properties and interests in the West. Some of the local leaders who have been elected with the backing of these 'pro-Russian' parties have already made it clear that they do not intend to collaborate with the invading forces.

But after the suspension of these parties, members of their local organizations and councils, as well as their active supporters, may be more inclined to collaborate with the Russians in the occupied areas.[10] Indeed, if they become convinced that they have no political future in Ukraine and rather face persecution, they may start looking towards Russia. This could fuel violence as masses begin searching for and punishing 'traitors' and strengthen Russian propaganda about Ukraine's 'Nazism' problem. There is already a worrying growth in reports about searches and arrests of opposition and left-wing bloggers and activists in Ukraine.

Today, Ukraine is facing an existential threat. The Ukrainian government needs to understand that moves such as these suspensions that alienate parts of the Ukrainian public – and make them question the intentions of their leaders – make the country weaker not stronger, and only serve the enemy.

26 October 2022

In late September, Russian President Vladimir Putin announced a 'partial' mobilization in Russia, as he forced through the annexation of four occupied regions in southeastern Ukraine after sham referendums. As many have pointed out, the draft broke an informal social contract between Putin and the Russian population, in which the Russian president provided not high but at least tolerable living standards and stability in exchange for political passivity.[11] Now, many expect the draft to change everything. Soon the corpses of poorly trained soldiers, sent as cannon fodder to the battlefield to stop the Ukrainian counter-offensive, will begin returning to their families, stirring public anger. According to this reasoning, this, along with the economic impact of sanctions, could result in popular unrest, which would necessitate further repression. The Kremlin would not be able to last long on sheer coercion. To score a military victory, Putin may be tempted to use a tactical nuclear weapon or some other wildly escalatory option that would likely deprive him of his unreliable allies in the world. Then he would either bury the whole world with him or be removed by a Russian elite scared for their own lives.

The problem with this line of thinking is that more repression is not the only option for Putin and is not the only basis of his regime. To understand the other direction he could take, it is important to look at the political economy dimension of recent developments. When declaring the 'partial' mobilization, Putin emphasized that drafted Russian soldiers would be paid the same as the contract soldiers who have been the backbone of the Russian forces in Ukraine so far. This means they should be paid at least $3,000 per month, depending on military rank, bonuses, insurance and a generous welfare package. This is about five to six times higher than the median wage in Russia. Drafting three hundred thousand, let alone more than one million soldiers – as some media reports have claimed may be the real target – would necessitate the redistribution of billions of dollars from the Russian state budget.

There were reports of chaos in the payment arrangements in the first weeks after the start of mobilization. However, at a meeting of Russia's Security Council on 19 October, Putin ordered that all problems with military wages be resolved, showing that the high remuneration for mobilized soldiers and support for their families is an important part of his strategy. Add to that the money flowing to the reconstruction of the ruined Mariupol and other heavily destroyed Ukrainian cities in the newly annexed regions of southeastern Ukraine. Currently, workers from across Russia are recruited for the reconstruction effort and are offered double the amount they would make at home. Even a non-qualified construction worker receives more than $1,000 a month.

Recently, Russian Deputy Prime Minister Marat Khusnullin said more than thirty thousand Russian workers are employed in the reconstruction of occupied Ukrainian territories, and that the government plans to increase the number to fifty to sixty thousand. In the next three years, the Russian budget is expected to allocate at least $6 billion for the reconstruction of the newly annexed Ukrainian territories. How much of it will not be lost to Russian crony capitalism remains to be seen.

There are also a lot of funds flowing into the military-industrial complex. As demand for weapons and munitions has increased significantly, the number of workers, as well as wages, has grown. At least partially, the growth in the military-industrial complex compensates for the decline of production in the industries dependent on Western components and suffering from sanctions. In other sectors, employees who have been drafted into the army have left jobs to be filled by new workers, which decreases unemployment.

All in all, the state expenditure for 'national defence' has already increased by 43 per cent since last year, reaching $74 billion. A planned cut for 2023 has been scrapped and instead Moscow plans to spend some $80 billion. The 'national security and law enforcement' expenses are also expected to increase by 46 per cent to $70 billion next year.

Looking at these developments, we see something like a military Keynesianism taking shape in Russia. Millions of Russians who are either mobilized to fight in Ukraine, employed in reconstruction or in the military industry or participating in the suppression of unrest in the occupied territories and at home, as well as family members, have turned into direct beneficiaries of the war. Among other things, this means the emergence of a positive feedback loop that did not really exist before. The Russian ruling elite started the war to pursue its own interests and it managed to get only ritual and passive support from the Russian population. However, this redistribution of state wealth through the military effort is creating a new basis for more active and conscious support within a significant section of Russian society, which now has a material stake in the conflict.

The fact that a full-scale invasion and occupation of a large part of the Ukrainian territory would require some fundamental changes in the Russian sociopolitical order was predictable even before 24 February. The Kremlin's strategy of combining coercion with bribing a significant part of the population has helped keep anti-war protests relatively small, as most Russians have obediently accepted the mobilization. The disproportionate number of people drafted from the poorer parts of Russia might have to do not only with the Kremlin's fear of protests from the more opposition-minded residents of the big cities but also with its calculation that the monetary incentives it offers would be of greater value to the residents of more deprived, peripheral regions.

The crucial question, of course, is for how long military Keynesianism will be sustainable in Russia. The classical imperialist positive feedback loops relied on technologically advanced industrial production. The conquered territories and colonies provided new markets and supplied the raw materials and cheap labour to expand production even more. The profits were then shared with the 'labour aristocracy' at home, who benefited from the imperialist expansion and subjugation. The bloc formed between the imperialist ruling classes and segments of the working classes became the basis of the hegemonic regimes and precluded social revolutions in Western metropolises. Whether Ukraine can provide any of the above for the Russian economy is highly questionable. Furthermore, many expect that the long-term impact of sanctions will cripple the Russian economy and lead to its primitivization.

That leaves the flow of petrodollars as the main source of funding to buy loyalty. That, however, depends on the successful reorientation to the non-Western markets and sufficient growth of China and India's economies to sustain the demand for Russian energy resources. No less important would be reforming Russian state institutions in order to manage revenues more efficiently, rather than lose them to incompetence and corruption. But if the Russian regime is capable of transforming and strengthening in response to the existential challenge rather than collapsing, it means that Russia could be ready for a longer and more devastating war.

Russian military Keynesianism contrasts sharply with the Ukrainian government's decision to stick to neoliberal dogmas of privatization, lowering taxes and extreme labour deregulation, despite the objective imperatives of the war economy. Some top-notch Western economists have even recommended to Ukraine policies that constitute what British historian Adam Tooze has termed 'warfare without the state'.[12] In a long war of attrition, such policies leave Ukraine even more dependent not only on Western weapons but also on the steady flow of Western money to sustain the Ukrainian economy. Making oneself fundamentally dependent on Western support may not be a safe bet, especially if your adversary is in it for the long haul.

7

NATO through Ukrainian Eyes

January 2023

Did Russia invade Ukraine to prevent further NATO encroachment on its western marches? Or was such agita merely a pretext? For those who take Vladimir Putin's 'legitimate security concerns' at face value, NATO is itself culpable for the war, by holding out the promise of Ukrainian membership while engaging in increasingly intensive military coordination with Kiev. By contrast, Atlanticist consensus rejects the issue altogether, on the grounds that every state has the right to determine its own foreign policy, not least accession to a purely 'defensive' alliance. Concerns voiced by two generations of Soviet and Russian leaders can thus be dismissed as a ploy, contrived to dissemble deep-seated imperialistic designs.

Whatever role NATO expansion played in bringing about war, Ukrainians' attitudes counted for little. The grim irony is not only that NATO was far from extending formal membership to Ukraine, but that there was not even evidence of a stable pro-NATO majority in the country. In a typically colonial style, commentators on all sides tended to homogenize Ukrainians, without regard for political diversity in a nation of forty million people. Contrary to the Kremlin's inclination to resolve Ukraine's geopolitical orientation within a small circle of Great Powers, Ukrainian officials have insisted on the principle 'nothing about Ukraine without Ukraine'. However, the problem is not only deciding 'without Ukraine', but also deciding 'for' a very diverse population as if all held identical opinions on the critical issues in question.

Beyond the global rivalry between the US and Russia, on the one hand, and regional Russo-Ukrainian relations, on the other, the conflict in Ukraine has always also been about internal political and cultural heterogeneity, which necessarily has a class dimension. NATO occupies a peculiar place in this history. For a middle-class civil society, joining the alliance is a necessary step towards 'Western integration', a catchphrase for an ersatz-modernization drive that entails adjustment not only to the demands of capitalist development but to the 'civilized world' itself. Other Ukrainians, less well positioned to benefit from this prospective *Gleichschaltung*, have been progressively stigmatized, silenced and repressed. The failure to achieve a pluralistic nation-building project for Ukraine has been disastrous, with consequences reaching far beyond its borders.

Did Ukrainians want to join NATO?

Non-alignment, ruling out entry into any military pact, was inscribed in the foundational documents of the state of Ukraine, the Declaration of Sovereignty (adopted 16 July 1990) and the Constitution (28 June 1996), following independence. And up until the tumultuous events of 2014, only a minority of Ukrainians favoured NATO membership. Surveys at the time show that support extended to no more than 20–30 per cent of the population, irrespective of how the issue was framed. By comparison, support for joining a supranational Union State alongside Russia and Belarus consistently hovered around 50–60 per cent (exceeding support for membership of the EU, although some Ukrainians did not see this as an either–or choice).[1]

Typical explanations of this muted enthusiasm point to ignorance of the alliance's post–Cold War mission and the persistence of negative stereotypes inherited from the communist era, coupled with the relatively low saliency of the issue insofar as accession was not on the agenda in the near feature.[2] But why should the legacy of communism weigh so heavily in this matter but not in others?[3] It was certainly not communist propaganda that caused support for NATO membership to plunge after the 2003 assault on Iraq to below 20 per cent in some continuous surveys.[4] That the US, not NATO, led the charge has little bearing; nobody was surprised when support for joining the Russia-led Collective Security Treaty Organization (CSTO) dropped in 2014 after the annexation of Crimea and the outbreak of hostilities in Donbass, despite the fact that the CSTO itself was not involved.

One thing that is clear, however, is that Ukrainian attitudes towards NATO reflected broader class divisions, in addition to pre-existing cleavages over regional and national identity. The more affluent and educated the person, the more likely they were to be pro-NATO.[5] In the years following independence, a post-Soviet professional middle class looked to 'Euro-Atlantic integration' for career opportunities, payoffs and political influence, while viewing the less affluent majority as incapable of making informed judgements on issues of foreign policy. Such a project of Westernization, undertaken by this privileged comprador elite, inevitably entailed a break with the 'backward' plebeian masses. As the latter clung to what stability they could in the chaotic aftermath of the collapse of the USSR, the former moved to counterfeit their particular interests as the national interest in toto.

Ukraine's cooperation with NATO began almost immediately after independence and deepened over time – although not without hesitation as to the end goal of acquiring membership, a project sometimes included and sometimes excluded from official national security statements. Oscillation was a leitmotif of the so-called 'multi-vector' strategy of balancing between Russia and the West. Rivals in Russia posed a threat to the ruling class of independent Ukraine, as tycoons in both countries vied to despoil what remained of Soviet-era infrastructure and state-owned enterprises. At the same time, like their Russian counterparts, Ukrainian political capitalists could not rejoin the Western elite without renouncing the selective benefits they obtained from the state – their major competitive advantage vis-à-vis transnational capital. The upshot was a cautious, opportunistic approach to security arrangements.[6]

More ardent NATO fans were to be found among the pro-Western, moderately nationalist neoliberals and conservatives organized politically into various 'national-democratic' parties. This camp, which also peopled the small but growing (thanks to Western donors) ranks of Ukraine's NGO-ized civil society, seized its chance after the Orange Revolution of 2004, which brought Viktor Yushchenko to power. It was Yushchenko, encouraged by George W. Bush, who pushed forward Ukraine's application for a NATO Membership Action Plan (MAP). Consulting the electorate was out of the question. On the eve of the April 2008 Bucharest Summit, at which it was declared that Ukraine and Georgia 'will become members of NATO', fewer than 20 per cent of Ukrainian citizens aspired to do so.[7] The rest were split between those who preferred an alliance with Russia and those attached to the non-aligned status quo; in late May and early June the previous year, the joint Ukraine–NATO 'Sea Breeze' naval exercise in Crimea had encountered significant protest, as locals greeted disembarking US Marines with cries of 'No to NATO in Ukraine!'[8]

Nor did the Ukrainian elite consolidate behind the membership bid. The issue envenomed Yushchenko's conflict with Yulia Tymoshenko and Viktor Yanukovych, who represented different fractions of Ukraine's political capitalists.[9] In 2007, then prime minister Yanukovych's refusal to sign off on the application for the MAP precipitated a full-blown governmental crisis, resolved only by snap parliamentary elections that September.[10] Even the Russia–Georgia war in 2008 did not substantially affect Ukrainian public opinion.[11] On winning the presidency in 2010, Yanukovych froze further rapprochement with NATO, all while persisting in negotiations over the EU Association Agreement that would prove to be his undoing. The EU, and with it the promise of higher living standards, was significantly more attractive in the eyes of Ukrainians than was NATO. In 2012–13, NATO polling numbers ran as low as 13 per cent, while upward of 40 per cent hoped to join the EU.[12] The same polls showed non-alignment to be the most popular security option, and the Union with Russia and Belarus the most desirable mechanism of economic integration, neck and neck with the EU.

It was not until 2014, with Russia's annexation of Crimea and the war in Donbass, that support for the NATO option increased dramatically, although it still was not embraced by a majority of Ukrainians.[13] Two factors contributed to the change in public opinion. Some previously sceptical Ukrainians now began to see NATO as a bulwark against Russian aggression. But no less importantly, the surveys did not include the most pro-Russian Ukrainian citizens concentrated in the territories no longer under Ukrainian government control – Crimea and parts of the Donetsk and Lugansk regions. Millions of citizens were thereby de facto excluded from the Ukrainian public sphere.[14] In the rest of Ukraine, backing for a military alliance with Russia (as well as economic integration) dropped sharply after 2014. However, most of those who were once inclined towards Russia did not transfer their allegiance to NATO. Rather, they switched to a non-aligned position, in the spirit of 'a plague on both your houses'.

Support for NATO in Ukraine has continued to vary geographically.[15] Before the 2022 invasion, a solid majority existed only in the western regions. There was, perhaps, a pro-NATO plurality in central Ukraine. But non-alignment prevailed in the east and south: the areas of Ukraine that would take the heaviest blow in the event of a clash with Russia. The correlation between Ukrainians' views on NATO and their different visions of Ukrainian national identity made the issue especially divisive. If many Ukrainians saw in NATO protection from a bellicose neighbour, many others worried that membership in the alliance would forfeit yet more sovereignty to the West,[16] increase tensions with Russia, aggravate internal divisions and potentially drag Ukraine into one of the US's 'forever' wars.[17]

Had Bush not defended opening the door to Kiev, over French and German objections, with reference to Ukrainian valour in Kosovo, Afghanistan and Iraq?[18]

Some evidence did indicate growing support for NATO membership in the wake of the election of Volodymyr Zelenskyi.[19] To start with, the new president – a Euro-Atlantic partisan, inaccurately besmirched as 'pro-Russian' by Ukrainian nationalists and international 'friends of Ukraine'[20] – somewhat 'de-toxified' the issue among eastern Ukrainian voters, and even more importantly, the Russian military build-up from the spring of 2021 raised alarm. All the same, it is doubtful whether a stable majority – as distinct from fleeting, conjunctural upticks in polling – existed even in the run-up to the invasion. As late as December 2021, polls suggested that non-alignment commanded a plurality of around 45 per cent.[21] NATO supporters probably would have prevailed in a referendum; however, even setting aside the limits of a 'yes' or 'no' response in dictating national security strategy, a vote under these conditions would not have included the millions of Ukrainian citizens in the Donbass and Crimea. If their opinions are taken into account (Ukraine has never formally abandoned the ambition to bring them back), the notion of a stable pro-NATO majority in Ukraine before the full-scale invasion is flawed.

East–West asymmetries

Scepticism towards NATO can be effaced only by downplaying or delegitimizing the internal diversity of Ukraine. Here, explanations that assume some roughly symmetrical 'East/West' political cleavage – whether based on ethnicity and language, national identity or historically constituted political cultures – mislead insofar as they overlook the profound *asymmetry* between the two main political blocs that emerged in independent Ukraine. The 'Western' camp rested on an alliance between the professional middle class and transnational capital, organized and ideologically articulated in the national-liberal civil society of NGOs and militant nationalist parties, and electorally represented by some fractions of Ukrainian political capitalists ('oligarchs') who rather opportunistically joined the camp.[22] The 'Eastern' camp – most political capitalists arrayed uneasily behind it – relied on the passive electoral support of industrial workers and public-sector employees, absent any genuine activist mobilization. The mediating civil society layer between the oligarchic 'leaders' and their rather apolitical voters was remarkably weaker within the 'Eastern' camp.[23]

This discrepancy explains why even though the 'Eastern' camp comprised a large minority or sometimes even the majority of Ukrainian citizens, its political and organizational resources paled in comparison with those available to Western-oriented nationalists and neoliberals, however unpopular the agendas they sought to impose. The constitutional amendment enshrining Ukraine's intention to join NATO and the EU, enacted in February 2019 by Zelenskyi's predecessor, Petro Poroshenko, must be understood in this light. Unsurprisingly, plaudits from national-liberal civil society did not prevent the incumbent president's devastating defeat only months later.

Once installed as president, however, Zelenskyi did not reverse the exclusionary nationalist drift of Poroshenko's rule, despite the expectations of a large part of his voters. Zelenskyi's civic nationalism remained shallow, paying lip service to diversity in the place of meaningful action. Beginning in 2021, the president increasingly targeted political opponents with threats and sanctions, went after their financial backers and banned most of the major opposition media. Squawks of disapproval from human rights organizations aside, these measures elicited no significant reaction from 'the West', in striking contrast to the repression of opposition elements in Russia and Belarus.[24] Few observers questioned the idea that persecution of so-called pro-Russian forces is inevitable or even legitimate in a country under the foreign threat. Fewer still considered whether depriving a large segment of the population of political and public representation made Ukraine weaker, rather than stronger, vis-à-vis Russia.

After the invasion

For adepts of the 'Western' nation-building project, Russia's invasion of Ukraine turned into an opportunity to transform the country in their own image. Of course, a full-scale invasion can be expected to have more profound effects than the eventful months of Euromaidan, the almost bloodless annexation of Crimea and localized combat in Donbass. It would be a bitter irony if Russian arms unified a NATO-oriented Ukrainian nation-state, something that pro-Western elites were unable to accomplish in the three decades after the dissolution of the USSR. But a closer look into the nature of this apparent unity invites doubt as to whether it will outlast the end of the conflict.

If anything could have been expected to follow from the Russian invasion, it was an embrace of NATO. A survey conducted in May 2022 duly found that 73 per cent of respondents wanted to see Ukraine to become an alliance member by 2030, although a significant minority of 27 per cent still preferred Ukraine to be non-aligned.[25] An August sample returned comparable figures.[26]

However, wartime polling suffers from a host of challenges. At the time of writing, surveys exclude not only the inhabitants of areas that the government in Kiev did not control before the invasion, but millions of refugees now living abroad. Among those forced to flee their homes, the majority come from the regions in southeastern Ukraine, again skewing the balance of reported opinion.[27] Canvassers struggle to reach the residents of Russian-occupied areas in the south of the country, while the wartime mobilization inescapably amplifies 'spiral of silence' effects, discouraging the expression of views that may be considered unpatriotic.[28] One poll that did include Ukrainians relocated abroad – a continuous panel survey via mobile applications, carried out by Gradus in April 2022 – turned up remarkable results. Slightly fewer than half of those polled countenanced Ukraine joining NATO, in response to an either–or choice; finer-grained questioning found that 24 per cent favoured NATO membership, as against 27 per cent for non-alignment (with security guarantees) and another third undecided.[29] Asked to reflect on the future, only 20 per cent mentioned accession to NATO as an 'inspiring thing', which was dwarfed by those who hoped for an end to the war, political and economic transformation, and improvement of their own material well-being, as well as EU member status for Ukraine (39 per cent).

Once reductive binary choices are dispensed with, superficial unity on foreign policy and security arrangements conceals a good deal of diversity. Another poll from May 2022 found 42 per cent endorsed neutrality for Ukraine on the condition of guarantees from the Western powers, while a roughly equivalent number (39 per cent) insisted on entering NATO no matter what.[30] Results like these suggest that only a minority see enrolment in the alliance as a matter of identity, whereas for many others their support is conditional and open to change, especially as a function of NATO's evolving role in the war. As demonstrated by a December 2022 poll, when provided a range of alternatives to choose from as the 'best option to guarantee the national security of Ukraine after the Russian aggression' – including strategic cooperation with the US or other allied states, development of Ukraine's own armed forces and non-aligned status with international security guarantees – joining NATO is the most popular option, but it still falls short of a majority (49 per cent).[31] In stark contrast with prevailing orthodoxy in both the US and Western Europe concerning war guilt, Ukrainians deliver more nuanced appraisals. A June 2022 survey commissioned by the *Wall Street Journal* discovered that although 85 per cent attributed 'a great deal' or at least 'some' responsibility for the 'ongoing conflict' to Russia, majorities also assign blame to the US (58 per cent), NATO (55 per cent) and the Ukrainian government (70 per cent).[32] Many no doubt reprove the Western powers for not admitting Ukraine to the alliance, sending weapons even earlier and preparing properly for the invasion. However, these were presumably not the chief concerns of the 35 per cent who assigned responsibility for the war to 'Ukraine's ultra-right nationalists'. Startlingly, a small but not insignificant minority of the Ukrainians polled (9 per cent) did not blame Russia at all.

Aside from doubts over the reliability of survey data, one must also take into account the intense cathexis of wartime patriotism, which does not necessarily promise more lasting, durable national unity. The enormous suffering and deadly risk the invasion imposed on practically every resident of Ukraine inevitably leads many to reject any premise that may be contaminated by enemy 'narratives', irrespective of the facts on the ground.[33] Initial success in resisting and repulsing the Russian military in large parts of the occupied territories fed hopes of total victory. Affective responses to the extraordinary stress of the war are evident in connection to not only complex issues of international politics, but also the simple facts of everyday life. Despite a 30 per cent fall in GDP, surging unemployment and regular power cuts due to the Russian attacks on the energy infrastructure, half as less Ukrainians despaired of the economic situation in December 2022 (28 per cent) as in pre-invasion polls a year prior (58 per cent in November 2021).[34] The percentage of those who report that living conditions are satisfactory for the majority of the population has likewise almost doubled over the same period.

The overall picture looks less like an expression of newfound unity under the leadership of pro-Western elites than a negative coalition against an external foe – a precarious, volatile solidarity, rather than a fundamental shift in political beliefs. Deeper divisions may be subsumed temporarily, but they threaten to return to the fore when the fighting ceases. This will be amplified by new cleavages between those who stayed in Ukraine, those who found refuge abroad, and those who remained in territories annexed by Russia and therefore in one way or another had to collaborate with the occupying authorities. Whatever the outcome on the battlefield, Ukrainian attitudes towards a post-war geostrategic settlement cannot be foretold. If recent history is any guide, they are unlikely to weigh too heavily in the calculations of political elites, whether at home or abroad.

8

Behind Russia's War Is Thirty Years of Post-Soviet Class Conflict

October 2022

Since Russian forces invaded Ukraine earlier this year, analysts across the political spectrum have struggled to identify exactly what – or who – led us to this point. Phrases like 'Russia', 'Ukraine', 'the West' or 'the Global South' have been thrown around as if they denoted unified political actors. Even on the left, the utterances of Vladimir Putin, Volodymyr Zelenskyi, Joe Biden and other world leaders about 'security concerns', 'self-determination', 'civilizational choice', 'sovereignty', 'imperialism' or 'anti-imperialism' are often taken at face value, as if they represented coherent national interests.

Specifically, the debate over Russian – or, more precisely, the Russian ruling clique's – interests in launching the war tends to be polarized around questionable extremes. Many take what Putin says literally, failing to even question whether his obsession with NATO expansion and his insistence that Ukrainians and Russians constitute 'one people' represent Russian national interests or are shared by Russian society as a whole. On the other side, many dismiss his remarks as bold-faced lies and strategic communication lacking any relation to his 'real' goals in Ukraine.

In their own ways, both of these positions serve to mystify the Kremlin's motivations rather than clarify them. Today's discussions of Russian ideology often feel like a return to the times of *The German Ideology*, penned by Karl Marx and Friedrich Engels in their youth, some 175 years ago. To some, the dominant ideology in Russian society is a true representation of the social and political order. Others believe that simply proclaiming the emperor has no clothes will be enough to pierce the free-floating bubble of ideology.

Unfortunately, the real world is more complicated. The key to understanding 'what Putin really wants' is not cherry-picking obscure phrases from his speeches and articles that fit observers' preconceived biases, but rather conducting a systematic analysis of the structurally determined material interests, political organization and ideological legitimation of the social class he represents. In the following, I try to identify some basic elements of such an analysis for the Russian context. That does not mean a similar analysis of the Western or Ukrainian ruling classes' interests in this conflict is irrelevant or inappropriate, but I focus on Russia partially for practical reasons, partially because it is the most controversial question at the moment and partially because the Russian ruling class bears the primary responsibility for the war. By understanding their material interests, we can move beyond flimsy explanations that take rulers' claims at face value and move towards a more coherent picture of how the war is rooted in the economic and political vacuum opened up by the Soviet collapse in 1991.

What's in a name?

During the current war, most Marxists have referred back to the concept of imperialism to theorize the Kremlin's interests. Of course, it is important to approach any analytical puzzle with all available tools. It is just as important, however, to use them properly. The problem here is that the concept of imperialism has undergone practically no further development in its application to the post-Soviet condition. Neither Vladimir Lenin nor any other classical Marxist theorist could have imagined the fundamentally new situation that emerged with the collapse of Soviet socialism. Their generation analyzed the imperialism of capitalist expansion and modernization. The post-Soviet condition, by contrast, is a permanent crisis of contraction, de-modernization and peripheralization.

That does not mean that analysis of Russian imperialism today is pointless as such, but we need to do quite a lot of conceptual homework to render it fruitful. A debate over whether contemporary Russia constitutes an imperialist country by referring to some textbook definitions from the twentieth century has only scholastic value. From an explanatory concept, 'imperialism' turns into an ahistorical and tautological descriptive label: 'Russia is imperialist because it attacked a weaker neighbour'; 'Russia attacked a weaker neighbour because it is imperialist', and so on. Failing to find the expansionism of Russian finance capital (considering the impact of sanctions on the very globalized Russian economy and the Western assets of Russian 'oligarchs'); the conquest of new markets (in Ukraine, which has failed to attract virtually any foreign direct investment (FDI), except for the offshore money of its own oligarchs); control over strategic resources (whatever mineral deposits lie in Ukrainian soil, Russia would need either expanding industry to absorb them or at least the possibility to sell them to more advanced economies, which is (surprise!) only severely restricted because of the Western sanctions); or any other typical imperialist causes behind the Russian invasion, some analysts still claim that the war may possess the autonomous rationality of a 'political' or 'cultural' imperialism. This is ultimately an eclectic explanation. Our task is precisely to explain how the political and ideological rationales for the invasion reflect the ruling class's interests. Otherwise, we inevitably end up with crude theories of power for the sake of power or ideological fanaticism. Moreover, it would mean that the Russian ruling class has either been taken hostage by a power-hungry maniac and national chauvinist obsessed with a 'historical mission' of restoring Russian greatness, or suffers from an extreme form of false consciousness – sharing Putin's ideas about the NATO threat and his denial of Ukrainian statehood, leading to policies that are objectively contrary to their interests.

I believe this is wrong. Putin is neither a power-hungry maniac, nor an ideological zealot (this kind of politics has been marginal in the whole post-Soviet space), nor a madman. By launching the war in Ukraine, he protects the rational collective interests of the Russian ruling class. It is not uncommon for collective class interests to only partially overlap with the interests of individual representatives of that class, or even contradict them. But what kind of class actually rules Russia – and what are its collective interests?

Political capitalism in Russia and beyond

When asked which class rules Russia, most people on the left would likely answer almost instinctively: capitalists. The average citizen in the post-Soviet space would probably call them thieves, crooks or mafia. A slightly more highbrow response would be 'oligarchs'. It is easy to dismiss such answers as the false consciousness of those who do not understand their rulers in 'proper' Marxist terms. However, a more productive path of analysis would be to think about why post-Soviet citizens emphasize the stealing and the tight interdependency between private business and the state that the word 'oligarch' implies.

As with the discussion of modern imperialism, we need to take the specificity of the post-Soviet condition seriously. Historically, the 'primitive accumulation' here happened in the process of the Soviet state and economy's centrifugal disintegration. Political scientist Steven Solnick called this process 'stealing the state'.[1] Members of the new ruling class either privatized state property (often for pennies on the dollar) or were granted plentiful opportunities to siphon off profits from formally public entities into private hands. They exploited informal relations with state officials and the often intentionally designed legal loopholes for massive tax evasion and capital flight, all while executing hostile company takeovers for the sake of quick profits with a short-term horizon.

Russian Marxist economist Ruslan Dzarasov captured these practices with the 'insider rent' concept, emphasizing the rent-like nature of income extracted by insiders thanks to their control over the financial flows of the enterprises, which depend on the relationships with the power holders.[2] These practices can certainly also be found in other parts of the world, but their role in the formation and reproduction of the Russian ruling class is far more important due to the nature of the post-Soviet transformation, which began with the centrifugal collapse of state socialism and the subsequent political-economic reconsolidation on a patronage basis. Other prominent thinkers, such as Hungarian sociologist Iván Szelényi, describe a similar phenomenon as 'political capitalism'.[3] Following Max Weber, political capitalism is characterized by the exploitation of political office to accumulate private wealth. I would call the political capitalists the fraction of the capitalist class whose main competitive advantage is derived from selective benefits from the state, unlike capitalists, whose advantage is rooted in technological innovations or a particularly cheap labour force. Political capitalists are not unique to the post-Soviet countries, but they are able to flourish precisely in those areas where the state has historically played the dominant role in the economy and accumulated immense capital, which is now open for private exploitation.

The presence of political capitalism is crucial to understanding why, when the Kremlin speaks about 'sovereignty' or 'spheres of influence', this is by no means the product of an irrational obsession with outdated concepts. At the same time, such rhetoric is not so much an articulation of Russia's national interest as a direct reflection of the Russian political capitalists' class interests. If the state's selective benefits are fundamental for the accumulation of their wealth, these capitalists have no choice but to fence off the territory where they exercise monopoly control – control not to be shared with any other fraction of the capitalist class.

This interest in 'marking territory' is not shared by, or at least not so important for, different types of capitalists. A long-running controversy in Marxist theory centred on the question of, to paraphrase Göran Therborn, 'what the ruling class actually does when it rules'.[4] The puzzle was that the bourgeoisie in capitalist states does not usually run the state directly. The state bureaucracy usually enjoys substantial autonomy from the capitalist class but serves it by establishing and enforcing rules that benefit capitalist accumulation. Political capitalists, by contrast, require not general rules but much tighter control over political decision-makers. Alternatively, they occupy political offices themselves and exploit them for private enrichment.

Many icons of classical entrepreneurial capitalism benefited from state subsidies, preferential tax regimes or various protectionist measures. Yet, unlike political capitalists, their very survival and expansion on the market only rarely depended on the specific set of individuals holding specific offices, the specific parties in power or the specific political regimes. Transnational capital could and would survive without the nation-states in which their headquarters were located – recall the seasteading project, comprising floating entrepreneurial cities independent of any nation-state, boosted by Silicon Valley tycoons like Peter Thiel. Political capitalists cannot survive in global competition without at least some territory where they can reap insider rents without outside interference.

Class conflict in the post-Soviet periphery

Whether political capitalism will be sustainable in the long run remains an open question. After all, the state needs to take resources from somewhere to redistribute them among the political capitalists. As Branko Milanović notes, corruption is an endemic problem for political capitalism, even when an effective, technocratic and autonomous bureaucracy runs it.[5] Unlike in the most successful cases of political capitalism, such as China, the Soviet Communist Party institutions disintegrated and were replaced by regimes based on personal patronage networks bending the formal facade of liberal democracy in their favour. This often works against impulses to modernize and professionalize the economy. To put it crudely, one cannot steal from the same source forever. One needs to transform into a different capitalist model in order to sustain the profit rate, either via capital investments or intensified labour exploitation, or expand to obtain more sources for extracting insider rent.

But both reinvestment and labour exploitation face structural obstacles in post-Soviet political capitalism. On the one hand, many hesitate to engage in long-term investment when their business model and even property ownership fundamentally depend on specific people in power. It has generally proven more opportune to simply move profits into offshore accounts. On the other hand, post-Soviet labour was urbanized, educated and not cheap. The region's relatively low wages were only possible due to the extensive material infrastructure and welfare institutions the Soviet Union left as a legacy. That legacy poses a massive burden for the state, but one that is not so easy to abandon without undermining support from key groups of voters. Seeking to end the rapacious rivalry between political capitalists that characterized the 1990s, Bonapartist leaders like Putin and other post-Soviet autocrats mitigated the war of all against all by balancing out the interests of some elite fractions and repressing others – without altering the foundations of political capitalism.

As rapacious expansion began to run up against internal limits, Russian elites sought to outsource it externally to sustain the rate of rent by increasing the pool of extraction. Hence the intensification of Russian-led integration projects like the Eurasian Economic Union. These faced two obstacles. One was relatively minor: local political capitalists. In Ukraine, for example, they were interested in cheap Russian energy, but also in their own sovereign right to reap insider rents within their territory. They could instrumentalize anti-Russian nationalism to legitimate their claim to the Ukrainian part of the disintegrating Soviet state, but failed to develop a distinct national development project.

The title of the famous book by the second Ukrainian president, Leonid Kuchma, *Ukraine Is Not Russia* (2003), is a good illustration of this problem. If Ukraine is not Russia, then what exactly is it? The universal failure of non-Russian post-Soviet political capitalists in overcoming the crisis of hegemony made their rule fragile and ultimately dependent on Russian support, as we have seen recently in Belarus and Kazakhstan.

The alliance between transnational capital and the professional middle classes in the post-Soviet space, represented politically by pro-Western, NGO-ized civil societies, gave a more compelling answer to the question of what exactly should grow on the ruins of the degraded and disintegrated state socialism, and presented a bigger obstacle to the Russia-led post-Soviet integration. This constituted the main political conflict in the post-Soviet space that culminated in the invasion of Ukraine.

The Bonapartist stabilization enacted by Putin and other post-Soviet leaders fostered the growth of the professional middle class. A part of it – for example, those employed in bureaucracy or in strategic state enterprises – shared some benefits of the system. However, a large part of it was excluded from political capitalism. These people's main opportunities for incomes, career and developing political influence lay in the prospects of intensifying political, economic and cultural connections with the West. At the same time, they were the vanguard of Western soft power. Integration into EU- and US-led institutions presented for them an ersatz-modernization project of joining both 'proper' capitalism and the 'civilized world' more generally. This necessarily meant breaking with post-Soviet elites, institutions and the ingrained, socialist-era mentalities of the 'backward' plebeian masses sticking to at least some stability after the 1990s disaster.

The deeply elitist nature of this project is why it never truly became hegemonic in any post-Soviet country, even when boosted by historical anti-Russian nationalism as it was in Ukraine – even now, the negative coalition mobilized *against* the Russian invasion does not mean that

Ukrainians are united around any particular positive agenda. At the same time, it helps to explain the Global South's sceptical neutrality when called on to solidarize with either a wannabe Great Power on a par with other Western Great Powers (Russia) or a wannabe periphery of the same Great Powers seeking not to abolish imperialism, but to join a better one (Ukraine). For most Ukrainians, this is a war of self-defence. Recognizing this, we should also not forget about the gap between their interests and the interests of those who claim to speak on their behalf, and who present very particular political and ideological agendas as universal for the whole nation – shaping 'self-determination' in a very class-specific way.

The discussion of the role of the West in paving the way for the Russian invasion is typically focused on NATO's threatening stance towards Russia. But taking the phenomenon of political capitalism into account, we can see the class conflict behind Western expansion, and why Western integration of Russia without the latter's fundamental transformation could never have worked. There was no way to integrate post-Soviet political capitalists into Western-led institutions that explicitly sought to eliminate them as a class by depriving them of their main competitive advantage: selective benefits bestowed by the post-Soviet states. The so-called 'anti-corruption' agenda has been a vital, if not the most important, part of the Western institutions' vision for the post-Soviet space, widely shared by the pro-Western middle class in the region. For political capitalists, the success of that agenda would mean their political and economic end.

In public, the Kremlin tries to present the war as a battle for Russia's survival as a sovereign nation. The most important stake, however, is the survival of the Russian ruling class and its model of political capitalism. The 'multipolar' restructuring of the world order would solve the problem for some time. This is why the Kremlin is trying to sell its specific class project to the Global South elites that would get their own sovereign 'sphere of influence' based on a claim to represent a 'civilization'.

The crisis of post-Soviet Bonapartism

The contradictory interests of post-Soviet political capitalists, the professional middle classes and transnational capital structured the political conflict that ultimately gave birth to the current war. However, the crisis of the political capitalists' political organization exacerbated the threat to them.

Bonapartist regimes like Putin's or Alexander Lukashenko's in Belarus rely on passive, depoliticized support and draw their legitimacy from overcoming the disaster of the post-Soviet collapse, not from the kind of active consent that secures the political hegemony of the ruling class. Such personalistic authoritarian rule is fundamentally fragile because of the problem of succession. There are no clear rules or traditions to transfer power, no articulated ideology a new leader must adhere to, no party or movement in which a new leader could be socialized. Succession represents the point of vulnerability where internal conflicts within the elite can escalate to a dangerous degree, and where uprisings from below have better chances of succeeding.

Such uprisings have been accelerating on Russia's periphery in recent years, including not just the Euromaidan revolution in Ukraine in 2014 but also the revolutions in Armenia, the third revolution in Kyrgyzstan, the failed 2020 uprising in Belarus and, most recently, the uprising in Kazakhstan. In the two last cases, Russian support proved crucial to ensure the local regime's survival. Within Russia itself, the 'For Fair Elections' rallies held in 2011 and 2012, as well as later mobilizations inspired by Alexei Navalny, were not insignificant. On the eve of the invasion, labour unrest was on the rise, while polls showed declining trust in Putin and a growing number of people who wanted him to retire. Dangerously, opposition to Putin was higher the younger the respondents were.

None of the post-Soviet, so-called *maidan* revolutions posed an existential threat to the post-Soviet political capitalists as a class by themselves. They only swapped out fractions of the same class in power, and thus only intensified the crisis of political representation to which they were a reaction in the first place. This is why these protests have repeated so frequently. The *maidan* revolutions are typical contemporary urban civic revolutions, as political scientist Mark Beissinger called them.[6] Based on massive systematic data, he shows that unlike social revolutions of the past, the urban civic revolutions only temporarily weaken authoritarian rule and empower middle-class civil societies. They do not bring a stronger or more egalitarian political order, or lasting democratic changes. Typically, in post-Soviet countries, the *maidan* revolutions only weakened the state and made local political capitalists more vulnerable to pressure from transnational capital – both directly and indirectly via pro-Western NGOs. For example, in Ukraine, since the Euromaidan revolution, a set of 'anti-corruption' institutions has been stubbornly pushed forward by the IMF, G7 and civil society. These have failed to present any major case of corruption in the last eight years; however, they have institutionalized oversight of key state enterprises and the court system by foreign nationals and anti-corruption activists, thus squeezing domestic political capitalists' opportunities for reaping insider rents. Russian political capitalists would have a good reason to be nervous with the troubles of Ukraine's once-powerful oligarchs.

The unintended consequences of ruling-class consolidation

Several factors help to explain the timing of the invasion as well as Putin's miscalculation about a quick and easy victory, such as Russia's temporary advantage in hypersonic weapons, Europe's dependency on Russian energy, the repression of the so-called pro-Russian opposition in Ukraine, the stagnation of the 2015 Minsk Accords following the war in Donbass and the failure of Russian intelligence in Ukraine. Here, I have sought to outline in very broad strokes the class conflict behind the invasion, namely between political capitalists interested in territorial expansion to sustain the rate of rent, on the one hand, and transnational capital allied with the professional middle classes – which were excluded from political capitalism – on the other.

The Marxist concept of imperialism can only be usefully applied to the current war if we can identify the material interests behind it. At the same time, the conflict is about more than just Russian imperialism. The conflict now being resolved in Ukraine by tanks, artillery and rockets is the same conflict that police batons have suppressed in Belarus and in Russia itself. The intensification of the post-Soviet crisis of hegemony – the incapacity of the ruling class to develop sustained political, moral and intellectual leadership – is the root cause for the escalating violence.

The Russian ruling class is diverse. Some parts of it are taking heavy losses as a result of Western sanctions. However, the Russian regime's partial autonomy from the ruling class allows it to pursue long-term collective interests independently of the losses of individual representatives or groups. At the same time, the crisis of similar regimes in the Russian periphery is exacerbating the existential threat to the Russian ruling class as a whole. The more sovereigntist fractions of the Russian political capitalists are taking the upper hand over the more comprador, but even the latter likely understand that, with the regime's fall, all of them are losing.

By launching the war, the Kremlin sought to mitigate that threat for the foreseeable future, with the ultimate goal of the 'multipolar' restructuring of the world order. As Branko Milanović suggests, the war provides legitimacy for the Russian decoupling from the West, despite the high costs, and at the same time makes it extremely difficult to reverse it after the annexation of even more Ukrainian territory.[7] At the same time, the Russian ruling clique elevates the political organization and ideological legitimation of the ruling class to a higher level. There are already signs of a transformation towards a more consolidated, ideological and mobilizationist authoritarian political regime in Russia, with explicit hints at China's more effective political capitalism as a role model. For Putin, this is essentially another stage in the process of post-Soviet consolidation that he began in the early 2000s by taming Russia's oligarchs. The loose narrative of preventing disaster and restoring 'stability' in the first stage is now followed by a more articulated conservative nationalism in the second stage (directed abroad against Ukrainians and the West, but also within Russia against cosmopolitan 'traitors'), as the only ideological language widely available in the context of the post-Soviet crisis of ideology.

Some authors, like sociologist Dylan John Riley, argue that a stronger hegemonic politics from above may help to foster the growth of a stronger counter-hegemonic politics below. If this is true, the Kremlin's shift towards more ideological and mobilizationist politics may create the condition for a more organized, conscious, mass-political opposition rooted in the popular classes than any post-Soviet country has ever seen, and ultimately for a new social-revolutionary wave. Such a development could, in turn, fundamentally shift the balance of social and political forces in this part of the world, potentially putting an end to the vicious cycle that has plagued it since the Soviet Union collapsed some three decades ago.

9

Ukrainian Voices?

December 2022

Recently, there has been much talk about the 'decolonization' of Ukraine. This is often understood as ridding the Ukrainian public sphere and the education system of Russian culture and language. The more radical decolonizers, also to be found in the West, would like to see the Russian Federation disintegrate into multiple smaller states – to finish the process of the collapse of imperial Russia that began in 1917 and was not completed in 1991, with the dissolution of the USSR. In the university context, it may also mean 'decolonizing' the thinking of the social sciences and humanities, whose approach to the whole post-Soviet region is seen as having been penetrated and distorted by a long-term form of Russian cultural imperialism.

When the biggest wave of decolonization in modern history took place after World War II, the focus was different. At that time, decolonization meant not just the overthrow of the European empires but also, crucially, building new developmentalist states in the ex-colonial countries, with a robust public sector and nationalized industries to replace the imbalances of the colonial economy through import-substitution programmes. The contradictions and failures of such strategies were explored in broadly

Marxian terms in theories of under-development, debt-dependency and world-system analysis. Today, 'decolonization' is proposed for Ukraine and Russia in a context in which neoliberalism has taken the place of state-developmentalist policies and post-structuralist 'postcolonial studies' have displaced theories of neo-imperialist dependency. National liberation is no longer understood as intrinsically linked to social revolution, challenging the basis of capitalism and imperialism. Instead, it happens in the context of the 'deficient revolutions' of the Maidan type, which neither achieve the consolidation of liberal democracy nor eradicate corruption. If they succeed in overthrowing authoritarian regimes and 'empowering' the NGO representatives of civil society, they are also liable to weaken the public sector and increase crime rates, social inequality and ethnic tensions.[1]

It is not surprising, therefore, that talk of Ukraine's 'decolonization' is so much about symbols and identity, and so little about social transformation. If what is at stake is the defence of the Ukrainian state, what kind of state is it? So far, Ukraine's 'decolonization' has not led to more robust state-interventionist economic policies but almost precisely the opposite. Paradoxically, despite the objective imperatives of the war, Ukraine is proceeding with privatizations, lowering taxes, scrapping protective labour legislation and favouring 'transparent' international corporations over 'corrupt' domestic firms.[2] The plans for post-war reconstruction read not like a programme for building a stronger sovereign state but like a pitch to foreign investors for a start-up; or at least, that was the impression given by Ukrainian ministers at the Ukraine Recovery Conference in Lugano last summer. Some naively hope that 'war anarchism', founded on the cherished horizontal volunteerism that has flourished since the Russian invasion, will substitute for the time-proven 'war socialism'.[3] More sober assessments warn of the conditions being created for state fragmentation and a political economy of violence. It remains to be seen what the Ukrainian government will do with the recently nationalized industrial assets of selected oligarchs – return them to their former owners, pay compensation or reprivatize them to transnational capital – but it is highly unlikely that they will form the backbone of a stronger post-war public sector. In all probability, they will remain rather limited measures responding to the crises in specific industries.[4]

Ukrainian 'decolonization' is thus reduced to abolishing anything related to Russian influence in culture, education and the public sphere. Against this, it amplifies the voices articulating Ukrainian distinctiveness. This is combined with attacks on – or, as in Zelensky's banning of eleven political parties in March 2022, the repression of – the voices of those who oppose this process or are simply labelled, usually misleadingly, as 'pro-Russian'. In this way, Ukraine's 'decolonization' becomes a version of (national-) identity politics – that is, a politics centred on the affirmation of belonging to a particular essentialized group, with a projected shared experience. Here – thanks to the increased global interest in Ukraine, but also to the physical relocation of Ukrainians to Western countries where they can enter more actively into international debates – Ukrainian scholars, intellectuals and artists face a dilemma. Either we allow ourselves to become incorporated as just another 'voice' in a very specific field of institutionalized identity politics in the West, where Ukrainians would be only the latest addition to a long queue of myriad other minority voices. Or, instead, starting from the tragedy of Ukraine, we set out to articulate the questions of global relevance, search for their solutions and contribute to universal human knowledge. Paradoxically, this requires a much deeper and more genuine engagement with Ukraine than happens now.

Recognition for whom?

The critics of contemporary identity politics point to a fundamental contradiction: 'Why do we look for recognition from the very institutions we reject as oppressive?'[5] The oppressive situations faced by women, Black people and others involve complex social relations, institutions and ideologies, reproduced within the warp and weft of capitalist relations. The

Black, gay and women's liberation movements that arose in the 1960s and '70s fought to challenge the oppressive social order as a whole. While those oppressive relations persist, the question of universal emancipation has long since disappeared; instead, contemporary identity politics serve to amplify the particular voices that are deemed to require representation solely on the basis of their particularity. Instead of social redistribution, this politics calls primarily for recognition within the institutions which are not themselves put into question.[6] Moreover, because the groups that identity politics tends to essentialize are always internally diverse, it inevitably amplifies the more privileged voices who are legitimated to speak on behalf of the oppressed group that they may not really represent. In this way, it tends to reproduce and even legitimate fundamental social inequalities.

Needless to say, it is not Russian recognition that Ukrainian identity politics is seeking. The idea of talking to Russians, even unambiguously anti-Putin and anti-war Russians, is constantly under attack. As one Ukrainian politician put it, 'good Russians do not exist'.[7] Instead, Ukrainian identity politics primarily targets the West, which is held to be culpable for allowing the Russian invasion, trading with Russia, 'appeasing' Putin's regime, providing insufficient support for Ukraine and reproducing Russian imperialist narratives about Eastern Europe.[8] Yet, if the West is to be blamed for Ukraine's suffering, it could relatively easily redeem itself by providing unconditional support for 'the Ukrainian' and unconditional rejection of 'the Russian'. For this politics, the problem is Russian imperialism, not imperialism in general. Ukraine's dependency on the West tends not to be problematized at all.

Ukrainians, then, should be accepted as an organic and indispensable part of the civilized Western world. Indeed, Ukrainians turn out to be not just the same as Westerners, but even better than them. Defending the frontier of Western civilization, dying and suffering for Western values, Ukrainians are more Western than those who live in the West.[9] However, if Ukrainians are valued primarily for being on the front line of the war with

Russia, what positive contribution might the country make, beyond being more consistently anti-Russian? Is it only about recognition within the same unchallenged Western structures, trying to be more of the same? Is there anything else, besides occasionally beating Russia on the battlefield? There are hints to be gleaned from both directions: the West looking at Ukraine and Ukrainians looking at the West. Notably, they talk about different things. The Western gaze on Ukrainian politics usually takes a dichotomizing form. The bad aspects, when they are not perceived as a direct result of Russia's malicious influence, derive mostly from the local elites and 'corruption'. The good sides come from Ukraine's civil society, which (surprise!) is usually strongly supportive of 'the West' while often being generously supported by Western donors and, of course, contributing to Western self-esteem.

Some even claim that the Russian invasion has had a positive democratizing effect on Ukraine.[10] Before, the talk was usually precisely the opposite: the repressive tendencies in Ukrainian politics were recognized, but the Russian threat was to blame. What could one expect from a country that suffered from external aggression? If only the story of wartime democratization were true. There is some survey evidence that more Ukrainians support democratic values in the polls; there is no less extensive evidence that Ukrainians still prefer a strong leader rather than a democratic system and do not tolerate wartime dissent.[11] Ukrainians responded to the invasion with a burst of mutual help and horizontal cooperation, but is that untypical for a society facing an existential threat? Whether and how Ukrainian volunteerism will be institutionalized after the war is a big question; the previous wave of volunteerism at the start of the Donbass war in 2014 turned out to be driven by informal personalist initiatives and did little to sustain an organized civil society.[12] Meanwhile, Ukrainian politics carries on in the background, shutting down opposition parties, monopolizing TV broadcasts, typically choosing not to punish vigilantism, expanding databases of 'traitors' – some funded by US donors – and attacking those who dissent from the patriotic consensus. Are we really now in a position to give lessons on democracy and civic activism? Some Ukrainian oligarchs have been weakened as rockets, drones and artillery rain down on their property, their TV stations broadcast government content and their loyal MPs vote in unison with the pro-presidential party. But even if they don't regain their power after the war, it seems much less likely that their place will be taken by the self-organized Ukrainian people than by transnational capital, Zelenskyi's personalistic regime and the thin layer of NGO civil society.

Or should the world learn from our economy? This is actually a view arising from the Ukrainian gaze on the West. The middle-class Ukrainian refugees who have been starting new lives in the EU this year circulate scathing stories on social media about old-fashioned European bureaucracy and 'poor' service. But what stand behind the 'better' Ukrainian service sphere are the lowest wages in Europe and ever-poorer protection of labour rights. Ukraine's digitalization has advanced, but this is a typical laggard's advantage: Ukraine was forced to digitalize because the state institutions have been so inefficient – another reason why so much volunteerism and international aid is needed. However, emergency responses are hardly a long-term solution.

That's about it. These are not Ukraine's unique advantages; this is not why the Western elite currently cares so much about Ukraine. There has indeed been something of a legitimacy deficit in the West, increasing over the past decade; its symptoms include declining rates of support for the traditional parties, the rise of populist movements and new direct-action protests – Black Lives Matter, #MeToo – by the oppressed. In a sense, all are responses to the crisis of representation. All are saying: 'You – politicians, global elites, whites, men – do not represent us. You cannot speak for us.' Historically, the major Western states have been quite successful in neutralizing these criticisms through the formalistic inclusion of selected members of the marginalized groups, a 'solution' which excluded any larger challenges to the existing order. From the universal viewpoint of the oppressed, this tokenistic solution was always deficient; it alleviated the representation crisis without solving it.

Today, the Ukrainian resistance is exploited in a broadly similar way, to give greater credibility to Western superiority. Ukrainians are presented as fighting and dying for what too many Westerners do not believe in anymore. The noble fight brings (literally) new blood to its crisis-ridden institutions, wrapped in increasingly identitarian 'civilizational' rhetoric. The Western leaders repeatedly call for unity against the Russian threat. Substantive differences with political regimes in Russia, China or Iran obviously exist. However, the representation of the war in Ukraine as an ideological conflict – of democracy against autocracy – works poorly. The inconsistencies of the treatment of Russia, on the one hand, and Turkey, Saudi Arabia and Israel, on the other hand, are too great. And Putin too has been trying to instrumentalize the 'decolonization' narrative, presenting the September 2022 annexation of southeastern regions of Ukraine as a righteous struggle against Western elites who robbed most of the world and continue to threaten the sovereignty and 'traditional' cultures of other states. But what can he offer to the Global South beyond recognizing its 'representatives' as equal to the Western elites, on the basis of their self-proclaimed identities? The Western elites are trying to save the fraying international order; the Russian elite is trying to revise it to get a better place in a new one. However, neither can clearly explain how exactly the rest of humanity wins from either outcome. This is what 'multipolarity' may look like – the multiplication of national and civilizational identities, defined in opposition to each other but lacking any universal potential.

Ukraine's universal significance

The question for Ukrainians is whether being a part of this self-defeating escalation of identity politics is really what we need. This year, there has been a huge surge of events, panels and sessions related to Ukraine, Russia and the war, and a high demand for 'Ukrainian voices' in these discussions. Certainly, Ukrainian scholars, artists and intellectuals should be included in international discussions – and not just those about Ukraine. The problem, however, is not the quantity but the quality of such inclusion. We have seen how outdated arguments – not least those of primordial nationalism, weirdly combined with teleological claims for the superiority of liberal democracy – are legitimated.[13] We can already see the tokenism phenomenon, typical of contemporary identity politics, when a symbolic inclusion of 'Ukrainian voices' does not mean revising the structures of knowledge aligned with Western elite interests, beyond sharpening their guilt for appeasing Russia. Furthermore, the formalistic representation of tokenized 'Ukrainian voices' helps silence other 'voices' from Ukraine that are not so easy to instrumentalize. Are we really to believe that the English-speaking, West-connected intellectuals, typically working in Kiev or Lviv, and who often even personally know each other, represent the diversity of the 40-million-strong nation?

The solution is obviously not to include even more 'voices' but to break with the fundamentally flawed logic of escalating national-identity politics. Earlier, a distinctly colonial relation emerged between Western and East European scholars, including Ukrainians. We used to be typically the suppliers of data and local insights to be theorized by the Westerners, who would then reap most of the fruits of international intellectual fame. The sudden interest in Ukraine and the 'decolonization' moment offers an opportunity to revise this relationship.

Identity politics is a self-defeating game. Being recognized just for our 'Ukrainianness' means we are going to be marginalized again with the next geopolitical realignment. Instead of claiming to be the 'voices' of a people we cannot truly represent – that is, be held accountable by them – we should aim to be included on the basis of the contributions we can make to the universal problems facing humanity in escalating political, economic and environmental crises. In-depth knowledge of Ukraine and the whole post-Soviet region can be especially helpful here because some of the most detrimental consequences of these crises have manifested themselves in our region, in the sharpest and most tragic forms.

For example, how can we discuss the contemporary civic revolutions that are breaking out around the globe at an accelerating speed without Ukraine – the country where three revolutions happened during the life of one generation and brought hardly any revolutionary changes? These revolutions embody the contradictions of poorly organized mobilizations with vague goals and weak leadership in the sharpest form: the same problems that populist responses to the Western crisis of political representation have encountered.[14] Oppositionist parties come to power amid high expectations of change but typically fail even to start any major reforms. For decades, Ukraine was dominated by the cynical politics of the rival 'oligarchs', with record-low levels of trust in government that eventually led a staggering 73 per cent of voters to turn to a TV star, a complete novice in politics. Does it sound familiar? Or what about the relevance of the notorious 'regional cleavage' between Ukraine's 'eastern' and 'western' regions to the concerns about the growing polarization in the United States or post-Brexit Britain? Ukrainians – and, of course, East Europeans in general – had been living with systematically underfunded public-health institutions long before the COVID pandemic made this a widely recognized problem.

These are just some of the topics that would allow a more productive deprovincialization of discussions of Ukraine. It should not make us vulnerable to charges of 'Ukrainesplaining' – the ungrounded expansion of regional-specific frameworks to contexts which they fit only poorly. During the formative years of the classical social sciences, a handful of countries served as paradigmatic cases to explore fundamental processes. England was a model for discussions of the emergence of capitalism, while France was the foremost example of the dynamics of social revolution. The concepts of Thermidor and Bonapartism helped to illuminate the dynamics of political regimes in many other countries. Italy gifted us with the concepts of passive revolution and fascism.

These were the models for the period of capitalism's progressive expansion and modernization. If now, however, the world is experiencing a multisided crisis with no way out, shouldn't we look for the paradigmatic cases in other parts of the world — those that have been experiencing similar crisis trends, earlier and deeper? For example, the country that jumped from the European agrarian periphery to the cutting edge of space exploration and cybernetics in the space of just two generations — and then, in the life of the next, turned into the northernmost country of the Global South, with the sharpest decline of GDP and a devastating war; the country that flew to the stars and may now be bombed into the Middle Ages. Thirty years ago, we believed that post-Soviet countries would catch up with Western Europe and that Ukraine would be like Finland or France. By the mid-1990s, we tempered our ambitions and aimed rather to catch up with Poland or Hungary. It would be an exaggeration to say that the West may yet be catching up with the self-destruction of the post-Soviet countries; but we could turn out to be your future, not the other way around.

The call to see Ukraine as a paradigmatic case of the far-reaching global crisis requires a completely different perspective on the country itself. It means abandoning the typical post-Soviet teleological liberal-modernization story — which, in the guise of 'decolonization', requires us to interiorize a far inferior colonial position. Instead, we need to recognize that we could be proud of having once been part of a universal movement. Ukraine was crucial to the greatest social revolution and modernization breakthrough in human history. Ukraine was where some of the most significant battles of World War II took place. Millions of Ukrainian civilians and soldiers in the Red Army contributed huge sacrifices to defeat Nazi Germany. Ukraine was a world-renowned centre of vanguardist art and culture. The mass murders and authoritarianism of the state-socialist regime are universally acknowledged; but to exploit them to depreciate the scale of Soviet achievements is to cast Ukrainian labour, blood and suffering as meaningless. Moreover, it allows Putin to continue instrumentalizing Soviet history not only for domestic but for global audiences, who watch the ongoing war through the eyes not of the Western elites but of those whom they have oppressed for centuries. We should claim our past in full to claim a better future. The narrow 'decolonization' agenda, reduced to anti-Russian and anti-communist identity politics, only makes it more difficult to voice a universally relevant perspective on Ukraine, no matter how many Ukrainians would sympathize with it.

Interview: Towards the Abyss

New Left Review, March 2022

Your research has focused on the transformations of the Ukrainian political field since the 2014 Maidan uprising. What type of rupture did this represent? What new forces entered the arena, and what happened to the old ones?

The Euromaidan was not a rupture in the sense of a social revolution. As my colleague Oleg Zhuravlev and I have written, it shared features with other post-Soviet uprisings and also with those of the Arab Spring in 2011.[1] These were not upheavals that led to fundamental social changes in the class structure – nor even in the political structure of the state. Instead, they were mobilizations that helped to replace the elites, but where the new elites were actually fractions of the same class. The *maidan* revolutions in Ukraine – the 2014 Euromaidan was the last of the three – were similar. These are, in a sense, deficient revolutions: they create a revolutionary legitimacy that can then be hijacked by agents who are not actually representative of the interests of the revolutionary participants. The Euromaidan was captured by several agents, all of whom participated in the uprising and contributed to its success, but who were very far from representing the whole range of forces involved or the motivations that drove ordinary Ukrainians to support Euromaidan. In this sense, while responding to the post-Soviet crisis of political representation, the Euromaidan also reproduced and intensified it.

Predominant among these agents were the traditional parties of the opposition, represented by, among others, Petro Poroshenko, who became president of Ukraine in 2014. These oligarchic parties were structured around a 'big man', on patron–client relations: lacking any other model, they reproduced the worst features of the Communist Party of the Soviet Union – heavy-handed paternalism, popular passivity – voided of its legitimating 'modernity project'. Another smaller but very important agent was the bloc of West-facing NGOs and media organizations, which operated more like professional firms than community mobilizers, with the lion's share of their budgets usually coming from Western donors. During the uprising, they were the people who created the image of the Euromaidan that was disseminated to international audiences; they were responsible primarily for the narrative about a democratic revolution that represented the civic identity and diversity of the Ukrainian people against an authoritarian government. They gained strength in relation to the weakening Ukrainian state, which was first disrupted by the uprising, then thrown into further disarray by Russia's annexation of Crimea and by the separatist revolt in Donbass, backed by Moscow – and by Ukraine itself becoming more dependent on the West.

Then there were the far-right groups – Svoboda, Right Sector, the Azov movement – which, unlike the NGOs, were organized as political militants, with a well-articulated ideology based on radical interpretations of Ukrainian nationalism, with relatively strong local party cells and mobilizations on the streets. Thanks to the violent radicalization of Euromaidan, and then to the war in Donbass, these far-right parties were armed and could pose a violent threat to the government.[2] When the Ukrainian state weakened and lost its monopoly over violence, the right-wing groups entered this space. Western states and international organizations also gained increasing influence, both indirectly – through their funding of civil-society NGOs – and directly, because they provided credit and military help against Russia, as well as political support. These were the four major agents that grew stronger after the Euromaidan – the oligarchic opposition, the NGOs, the far right and Washington–Brussels.

And those who lost?

Those who lost power were, first, the sections of the Ukrainian elite – let's call them political capitalists, in the Weberian sense: exploiting the political opportunities their offices provided for profit-seeking – organized in the Party of Regions, which backed Viktor Yanukovych. After the Euromaidan, the party collapsed. These oligarchs, as they are usually called, were politically reorganized; but they retained control over some of the crucial sectors of the Ukrainian economy, so the Forbes list of the richest people in Ukraine remained amazingly stable. Before and after the Euromaidan revolution, the only person in the Top Ten list who made a career change was Poroshenko – a sign of how little change there was in the way the economy was working.

The other significant actor that lost out was the Communist Party of Ukraine (CPU). The left in general was badly affected, but the communists specifically were banned in 2015, under the laws on decommunization. These were the legal grounds for suspending the activities of the CPU, and also some of the marginal communist parties. In 2012, the CPU won 13 per cent of the vote, so it was a considerable part of Ukrainian politics. In 2014, they didn't get into parliament, thanks to the loss of Crimea and the Donbass, which were their electoral strongholds. And the next year, they were suspended.

In the interview you gave New Left Review *in 2014, you described how in the political struggles of 2004–14, the Orange parties would try to pull the Constitution towards a more parliamentary setup, and the Party of Regions would pull it back to a more presidential one.*[3] *What happened after 2014 to the constitutional balance, and the relative importance of parliament and president?*

After 2014, they rolled back to the more parliamentary–presidential model that worked after the 'Orange Revolution', and which Yanukovych cancelled in 2010 soon after he was elected president. On the formal level, in 2014, the president was weakened and parliament was supposedly stronger. The figure of the prime minister, who was chosen by the parliamentary deputies, became more important. But what did not change was the 'neopatrimonial' regime, as it is often called in the literature of post-Soviet studies: the informal patron–client relations that dominate politics. It is quite normal to speak of clans in this regard – to say someone is in the 'clan of Poroshenko', or the 'clan of Yanukovych'. These informally structured groups, whose relations are hidden from the public, have more influence on how real politics works in our country than the formal clauses of the Constitution. So despite the fact that the position of the presidency was formally weakened, Poroshenko was still the most influential politician in the country, able to push more or less what he wanted through parliament.

How did the composition of the parliament change in 2014?

There was a major change with the October 2014 parliamentary elections. Five pro-Maidan parties formed the ruling coalition – Poroshenko's party, Arseniy Yatsenyuk's People's Front, Yulia Tymoshenko's Fatherland and two others. It had a constitutional majority to begin with; but then, very quickly, the coalition started to crumble. Poroshenko did not want to recognize the collapse of the coalition because that would mean having to hold new elections, in which his party would perform worse than in 2014. And so, for several years, it was more like a conjunctural coalition, where his people had to manage the problem of getting majority votes.

What was Poroshenko's agenda?

When he was elected in 2014, Poroshenko wasn't seen as a representative of the radical wing of Euromaidan. But he was operating in the context of the new nexus of post-Maidan forces, in which, as I've said elsewhere, the interaction of oligarchic pluralism with a civil society that lacked institutionalized political or ideological boundaries between the West-backed NGOs and the far right, combined with the practically absent left wing, led to a process of nationalist radicalization.[4] The competing oligarchs exploited nationalism in order to cover the absence of 'revolutionary' transformations after the Euromaidan, while those in nationalist-neoliberal civil society were pushing for their unpopular agendas thanks to increased leverage against the weakened state.

Poroshenko promised before the elections that he would quickly establish peace in Donbass, and some perhaps voted for him for that reason. But within a few weeks, he had made a U-turn: instead of starting the negotiations with the separatists, he intensified the Anti-Terrorist Operation against them. The idea was to try to take over Donbass militarily. That strategy was defeated by the covert intervention of the Russian Army in August 2014, and that's how the Minsk process started, first in September, and then in February 2015, after another escalation and defeat of the Ukrainian forces. The Minsk agreements specified a ceasefire, Ukrainian recognition of local elections in the separatist-controlled areas, the transfer of control over the border to the Ukrainian government and a special autonomy status for Donbass within Ukraine, including the possibility of institutionalizing the separatist armed forces.

Who were the people standing up in favour of the Minsk Accords, and who was against? If this was the one chance of a peaceful settlement, why were they never implemented?

The people who were openly supportive were the opposition segment — mainly the parties that were the successors to the Party of Regions, which were oriented towards the eastern and southern voters, particularly citizens in the Ukraine-controlled parts of the Donbass, for whom the implementation of the Accords heralded the end of the war. For many other parties, Minsk was, at best, something that Russia had forcibly imposed on Ukraine. The argument was: we needed to stick with Minsk, because if Ukraine were to withdraw from the Accords, the West might lift the post-2014 sanctions against Russia. But at the same time, they were quite openly saying that they were not going to implement the political clauses of the Minsk Accords. Many argued that a politically integrated Donbass could block Kiev being able to implement a future Euro-Atlantic integration course, despite there being no mention in the Accords of such a veto. The only leverage Donbass would acquire would be the ability to blackmail Ukraine with the threat of secession, which would be easier to pull off than it had been in 2014. There was no discussion of how practically to prevent this. The Kiev government would also have had to discuss details of autonomy status with the leaders of the Donbass republics, whom they only ever referred to as 'terrorists' or 'Kremlin puppets'. The general logic of the Minsk Accords demanded recognition of significantly more political diversity in Ukraine, far beyond the bounds of what was acceptable after the Euromaidan. So, Russia accused Ukraine of lacking any desire to implement the political clauses of the Accords. Ukraine accused Russia and the separatists of violating the Accords by organizing local elections themselves and by distributing Russian passports among Donbass residents. Meanwhile, the death toll in Donbass grew.

Although in the end it appeared to be Putin who put an end to the Minsk Accords by recognizing the independence of the Donetsk and Lugansk People's Republics in February 2022, there had been multiple statements from Ukrainian top officials, prominent politicians and those in professional 'civil society' saying that implementing Minsk would be a disaster for Ukraine, that Ukrainian society would never accept the 'capitulation', it would mean civil war. Another important factor was the far right, which explicitly threatened the government with violence should it try to implement the Accords. In 2015, when parliament voted on the special status for Donetsk and Lugansk, as required by Minsk, a Svoboda Party activist threw a grenade into a police line, killing four officers and injuring, I think, about a hundred. They were showing they were ready to use violence.

How much did the fighting in the Donbass dominate the politics of this whole period? In the West, it was portrayed at the time as just another frozen conflict, although the casualty figures are quite high – some 3,000 civilian deaths. Was it on the TV news every evening?
It was a very important issue, of course. There was no stable ceasefire before 2020, so practically every day there were shellings or shootings, someone would be killed on the Ukrainian side or on the separatist side. Reports about casualties and shellings were regular news items. But only a minority of Ukrainians, besides Donbass residents and refugees, were directly affected by the war.

Putin claims the hard right dominated the Ukrainian forces in the Donbass.
They never dominated there, no. They were definitely a minority of the units. Some claim the Azov battalion was one of the most combat-ready units in the National Guard; perhaps so for a period in 2014–15, but not necessarily afterwards. I haven't studied the military in the Donbass closely, so these evaluations could be wrong. But what I know for sure is that Azov was definitely special; there was nothing else like it – a unit with a political agenda, affiliated to a political party, to a paramilitary organization, to summer camps training children, starting to develop an international strategy, inviting the Western far right to come to Ukraine – 'let's fight together' – creating a kind of 'Brown International'. *Die Zeit* published a major investigative article which situated Azov at the centre of the global extreme-right networks. But Azov was just one regiment.

Most of the Ukrainians who were fighting in the Donbass were not in politicized units.

But there was another phenomenon. Azov was integrated into the National Guard structure under the Ministry of the Interior, headed for years by Arsen Avakov, another of the pro-Euromaidan oligarchs. There were other armed factions that originated from the Right Sector, the radical nationalist coalition that became famous during the Euromaidan, that were not integrated, but which coordinated with the Ukrainian Army – what we might call wild groups that could do things the army command would prefer not to do. But even those groups were a small part of the Ukrainian forces fighting in Donbass.

What was the role of the deep state in this period? Did civic freedoms grow or shrink under the post-Maidan government?

One of the main narratives about post-Euromaidan Ukraine was the rise of an inclusive civic nation, finally unifying the east and west of the country, and a vibrant civil society pushing for democratizing reforms. Together with Oleg Zhuravlev, I have shown that the unifying trends were paralleled by polarizing trends; that the post-Euromaidan civic nationalism did not undermine but empowered ethnic nationalism; that inclusion and expansion of democracy for some meant exclusion and repression for others.[5] In this process of redefining what 'Ukraine' is about politically, a large tranche of political positions supported by many Ukrainians were moved beyond the boundaries of acceptability, according to this new articulation of the Ukrainian nation. So, if before 2014, 'pro-Russian' meant a large political camp supporting Ukraine's integration into Russia-led international organizations such as the Eurasian Union – or even joining the Union State with Russia and Belarus – after this camp collapsed in 2014, the 'pro-Russian' label was inflated and often used to stigmatize positions such as support for Ukraine's non-aligned status and pragmatic cooperation with both the West and East, as well as scepticism about Euromaidan outcomes, opposition to decommunization or restrictions on the use of the Russian language in Ukraine's public sphere.

So, a wide range of political positions supported by a large minority, sometimes even by the majority, of Ukrainians – sovereigntist, state-developmentalist, illiberal, left-wing – were blended together and labelled 'pro-Russian narratives' because they challenged the dominant pro-Western, neoliberal and nationalist discourses in Ukraine's civil society. Of course, not only was the stigmatization symbolic, but it could lead to online targeting campaigns, often initiated by 'patriotic' bloggers who made their public careers by identifying and harassing the 'enemies within' and which were amplified by civil society or paid internet bots. Occasionally, it ended in actual physical violence, usually conducted by radical nationalist groups. In the end, it helped to legitimate sanctioning the opposition media and some politicians in 2021.

So, this ideological shift principally represented a move towards a nationalist, anti-Russian agenda?

There were other groups that were also specifically targeted by the far right, like feminists, LGBT, Roma people, the left. By 2018–19, when I was still in Kiev and involved in organizing leftist media and conference projects, we were having to operate in a kind of semi-underground manner, never publishing the location of our 'public' events, with very careful preliminary checking of everyone who registered for events to see whether they might be provocateurs of some kind, people from the far right who had come to disrupt the event.

What did the Poroshenko administration actually achieve?

Poroshenko had moved increasingly towards the nationalist agenda by the end of his rule. Where the post-Maidan government actually got most done was in the ideological sphere: decommunization; empowering a nationalist historical narrative; Ukrainianization; restrictions on Russian cultural products; establishing the Orthodox Church of Ukraine independent of

Moscow (but subservient to the Constantinople Patriarchate). These were the planks that the Ukrainian hard right had campaigned on before the Euromaidan uprising; and although the nominal far-right politicians were not present in the post-Euromaidan governments in any significant way, this became the ruling agenda. But it would be simplistic to say that these were the positions of the far right alone, because they were legitimized within the broader bloc of national-liberal civil society. Demands that before the Euromaidan were seen as very radical suddenly became universalized, at least on the level of what we might call the activist public, although they were often not actually supported by the majority of society.

Another issue was symbolic identification with Euro-Atlantic integration. Ukraine's 1996 Constitution affirmed the principle of non-alignment. But starting from 2014, Poroshenko and his allies pushed for a change to this, which they could achieve thanks to the constitutional majority of the pro-Maidan parties. The constitutional amendments were passed by parliament in 2018 and signed into law by Poroshenko in early 2019 as a part of his electoral campaign. So now, in a country that may never become a member of NATO, the Constitution says that the state's 'strategic course' is full membership of NATO and the EU.

Before the 2019 elections, Poroshenko also campaigned heavily on the language issue; he pushed laws that significantly restricted the use of Russian language in the public sphere and education. By the time of the elections he was indeed seen as the leader of the nationalist cause. It was not surprising that he lost so heavily with this agenda in 2019, when Zelenskyi won by 73 to 25 per cent.

Why would Poroshenko fight an election campaign on these issues if they were so unpopular?
The dynamics of the deficient Euromaidan revolution could be behind this poor and puzzling choice. Poroshenko has never been an ideologically committed nationalist. He co-founded the Party of Regions and served as a

minister in Yanukovych's government; there have been scandals about the fact that his family speaks Russian at home, that he continued to do business in Russia after 2014. Following Euromaidan, Poroshenko was trapped between two opposing agendas: on the one hand, increasingly popular, though disorganized and inarticulate, expectations of post-revolutionary change; on the other, unpopular yet articulate and powerful demands from national-liberal civil society. Nationalist radicalization of the ideological sphere was, for Poroshenko, an easier way of delivering some 'revolutionary' change than proceeding with reforms that would have undermined the competitive advantages of his own faction among the political capitalist class. Appeals to nationalism also served to silence 'unpatriotic' criticism and to divide the opposition. When the Rada (the Ukrainian parliament) voted to change the Constitution regarding NATO and the EU, support for NATO was at about 40 per cent in Ukrainian society. So, this was not something that was pushed by the majority of voters, or that answered to a logic of 'we must do something popular before the election'. Poroshenko was pushing projects that were popular among the activist citizens – but not the majority of voters.

Similarly with 'decommunization'. Once the government had defined what this actually meant, polls showed that Ukrainians were not very interested in renaming the streets and cities or banning the Communist Party. At the same time, they were not ready to defend the Communist Party, because they did not see it as particularly relevant to their politics. But they were not supporters of decommunization either; they were passively against it, though not actively resisting it. The legitimacy of this agenda within the activist civil-society public was much higher than within Ukrainian society at large.

How did Ukraine's ideological and geographical divisions evolve in the post-2014 period? What happened, for example, in a traditionally Russia-oriented city like Kharkov?

Up until the Russian invasion, Kharkov hadn't changed that much. The Russian invasion is now changing the perceptions of Ukrainians, but this is very recent. What emerged after 2014 in Kharkov, and in the larger cities of the southeast, was a somewhat stronger middle-class, civil-society layer, with an outlook much like, let's say, western Ukrainian politics, but in contrast to – again, as I've explained before, this is a misleading and stigmatizing label – the 'pro-Russian' attitudes of the majorities in those cities. There was a disjunction between the activist citizens, who were taking part in rallies, writing for the press, blogging, Facebooking, and the people who were coming to the voting booths and electing the mayors, the local councils. The Mayor of Kharkov, Hennadiy Kernes, was shot in the back by some sniper in 2014 and seriously injured – he was in a wheelchair – but he continued to be re-elected until his death in 2020. Right after the Euromaidan, he went to Russia and maybe consulted with people there. He came back and took a position loyal to Ukraine – he didn't support the separatist revolt. He was quite popular in Kharkov and won significant support; he didn't have any real competition. Another striking fact: according to the opinion polls, outside the western regions, pro-nationalist attitudes had a very clear correlation with affluence: the higher people's incomes were, the more nationalist and pro-Western their views. In the western regions, there was no such correlation – nationalism had become rooted among the wider layers of society. But in the central, eastern and southern regions, the more middle-class you were, the more nationalistic and pro-Western you were likely to be.

Would you correlate that to other sociological differences between western and eastern Ukraine?

It's a question that still needs a lot of research, because it relates not only to how Ukrainian civil society was emerging, but to post-Soviet civil societies in general. For the layers who were protesting against Lukashenko, against Putin, but were unable to mobilize the majority of their societies against the authoritarian rulers, partially it involves a class divide; but in Ukraine it also overlaps with national identity and regional divides. In the western regions, you wouldn't see this class difference, because that kind of nationalism had been domesticated there for many decades. But in other places, Ukrainian nationalism was more of a middle-class phenomenon – which is of course very different from Western European nationalism, which at present is more working-class.

How does Europeanism fit in?
In the post-Soviet countries, again, Europeanism means something different. Pro-EU people in Western Europe would definitely keep a distance from the far right. But in the post-Soviet countries, this unusual mixture of nationalism, neoliberalism and pro-EU attitudes can work very well, as an ideology of the activist public.

What sort of alternative did Zelenskyi offer in 2019, compared to Poroshenko?
The 2019 elections were unprecedented. Ukrainian election results are usually very close: when Yanukovych won against Tymoshenko in 2010, for example, there were just three points between them: it was 49 to 46 per cent. The difference between Yushchenko and Yanukovych in 2004 was also very small, which allowed Yanukovych to steal the election – kick-starting the Orange Revolution. But by 2019, Poroshenko had huge disapproval ratings. Nearly 60 per cent of Ukrainians were saying they would never, ever vote for him. So Zelenskyi was able to unite a huge majority against Poroshenko; and what seemed even more hopeful was that Zelenskyi was winning in almost every region in Ukraine, except the three Galician regions in the west where nationalism was strongest, and where Poroshenko won. And so, there was some hope that Ukraine might finally be united. On the left, many did have hopes that with Zelenskyi there would be more space to breathe. I don't regret supporting him in 2019; I still think that was the right thing to do. Whatever happened next,

Zelenskyi's landslide alone undermined consolidation of Poroshenko's authoritarianism. It was also a huge blow to national-liberal civil society, which had rallied around Poroshenko, and felt quite disoriented when it appeared in the '25 per cent' camp of the political minority, after claiming for several years that the whole nation was united around its agenda. It also created political momentum to claim that the interests of the actual majority in Ukraine were not represented by the people speaking on behalf of the nation, which the old and new opposition parties attempted to seize.

How did the Zelenskyi government unfold?

After Zelenskyi won the presidential election in April 2019, he called snap parliamentary elections for July. It was a smart move because his Servant of the People Party, which had been created from scratch, won an overall majority – again, this was unprecedented in Ukrainian post-Soviet politics – so he was able to concentrate power in the central authorities. There were discussions about whether to have snap local elections as well; mayors play an important role in Ukrainian politics, and Zelenskyi's party would then have complete control if he tried to take some sensitive decisions, like, for example, implementing the Minsk Accords. But having snap local elections was more difficult to justify from a legal point of view. The success of the first prisoner exchanges between Ukraine, Russia and the Donbass in September 2019 contributed to his popularity, because it seemed that Ukrainian politics might be moving in a different direction. Zelenskyi had over 70 per cent approval ratings and a high level of trust in the polls. There was a window of opportunity to move forward with the Minsk Accords; there were active discussions of the so-called Steinmeier Formula that would provide an algorithm on how to implement the Accords. They were able to agree a temporary ceasefire which at least lasted for a significantly longer period than earlier ones had.

Then what happened?

It very soon became clear that not only was Zelenskyi's party not a real party, that this populist leader never had a populist movement behind him, but that he didn't even have a real team that was capable of proceeding with any consistent policies. His first government lasted for about half a year. He then fired his chief of staff, and there was continual turnover in ministerial positions. The lack of a serious team meant that Zelenskyi quite quickly fell into the same trap as Poroshenko, prey to the most powerful agents in Ukrainian politics: the oligarchic clans, the radical nationalists, liberal civil society and the Western governments, all pushing for their specific agendas, and the inflated mass expectations about radical changes after an 'electoral Maidan' that finally brought 'new faces' to the government. Within this trap, Zelenskyi was trying to build his own 'vertical of power', a typical informal 'chain of command' in post-Soviet politics. But he was not especially successful in that. Possibly we could analyse it as a kind of weak Bonapartism or Caesarism: an elected leader who tried to overcome these cleavages – attack the left, attack the right, attack the nationalists, attack the 'pro-Russians' – but did so quite erratically, and without consolidating his regime, ended up creating a mess and alienating many powerful figures in Ukrainian politics by the start of 2022.

Who are the people whom he has appointed to the key positions: the minister of the economy, minister of defence, foreign affairs, and so on? Do they come from his own party, or somewhere else?

His own party was created in a different way, so it was not of much use when filling ministerial positions. In the first government, there were many people from pro-Western NGOs. But Zelenskyi soon saw that they were not actually competent to run the Ukrainian economy. People with whom Zelenskyi had worked in TV – producers, actors, his personal friends – took some of the important positions. For example, the head of counter-intelligence is someone who was personally connected to Zelenskyi.[6] Later he took on people who had less of a pro-Western NGO profile, but offered some basic competence in government. Sometimes they were seen as connected to the oligarchic groups – for example, the prime minister, Shmyhal, worked for some time for Akhmetov. It is unlikely that he was under the influence of Akhmetov; but at that moment he was seen as a sign of a 'normal' politics returning to Ukraine: we are getting rid of those incompetent guys from NGOs, and starting to get more real functionaries into the government.

Zelenskyi was still in the process of creating a real team, with people coming from different sources – sometimes connected to the West, sometimes connected to himself, sometimes to oligarchic groups. By the start of the war, it was not yet clear that he had actually managed to build that 'vertical of power'. It was beginning to look more and more of a mess; and quite dangerous. From Putin's perspective, if Ukraine is in a mess, run by a weak and incompetent president, then isn't this a good time to achieve his goals?[7]

What happened to progress on the Minsk Accords?

Poroshenko and the nationalists had begun a so-called anti-capitulation campaign in 2019, protesting against implementation of the Minsk Accords, although they didn't have much backing. According to the polls, only a quarter of Ukrainians supported it, and almost half explicitly said they didn't. At the same time, Azov and other far-right groups were disobeying Zelenskyi's orders, sabotaging the disengagement of Ukrainian and separatist forces in Donbass. Zelenskyi had to go to a village in Donbass and parlay with them directly, even though he is the commander in chief. The 'moderate' anti-capitulation people could use the protests of the hard right to say that implementation of the Minsk Accords would mean a civil war because Ukrainians wouldn't accept this 'capitulation', and so there would be some 'natural' violence.

You've said that the hard-right groups were actually quite small, while Poroshenko had just been electorally annihilated. What else prevented Zelenskyi from carrying out his mandate?

The prospect of nationalist violence was real. But the question remains: why didn't Zelenskyi build an internal and international coalition in support of the Minsk Accords? Explicit and active support for the full implementation of the Accords by Western governments would have been a powerful signal to pro-Western civil society. Some people would say that by 2019 the Accords were unpopular – although they did have majority support in 2015, when they were signed, and there was a hope for peace. But by 2019 people were seeing them as ineffective at changing anything in the Donbass. However, neither Poroshenko nor Zelenskyi had ever seriously campaigned to increase the popularity of the Accords as much as they actually campaigned for the no less controversial and unpopular land market reform or various nationalist initiatives. Finally, France and Germany were not that active in pushing Ukraine to do more about the Accords and the Obama and Trump administrations certainly did not support the agreement as they could have.

What were the actual differences in policies between the Poroshenko and Zelenskyi presidencies, in retrospect? Other than the settling of political scores, would it be correct to say there was a substantial continuity between the two?

Yes, that's correct. There were expectations that Zelenskyi might revise the language law, to allow a greater presence of Russian in Ukraine's public sphere; that he might make real progress in implementing Minsk. Before the war, Zelenskyi failed in everything. Poroshenko was actually more capable of resisting some of the international institutions' demands – specifically the International Monetary Fund's pressure for market prices on gas, which Ukrainian governments always tried to block because it was hugely unpopular – especially with older people, for whom the price increase would be a heavy blow, and who vote in large numbers. Zelenskyi also pushed through a land market reform, which has been a big question since

Ukrainian independence and very unpopular; over 70 per cent of Ukrainians were against some of the clauses.

Was that the most important social and economic change that Zelenskyi has made, introducing land reform?

Yes, that was one of the most important, although he hedged it with restrictions, knowing it was unpopular. So at first, only Ukrainian citizens can start buying land, and then – maybe after a referendum – they might allow foreigners to buy it. But, nonetheless, he started the process, which had been stalled for thirty years. By the start of 2021, Zelenskyi had lost much of his popularity. The Opposition Platform – a successor to the Party of Regions and the runner-up in 2019 – was ahead of the Servant of the People party in some polls.

You've said that the ceasefire in the Donbass broke down at the end of 2020. What were the key steps that followed?

There are still many puzzles about the war and how it all started. Of course, the international dimension of NATO expansion and Russian imperialism, as well as the Kremlin's shifts in response to the latest wave of post-Soviet uprisings – in Armenia (2018), Belarus (2020), Kazakhstan (2022) – are all very important parts of the story. Putin's conviction that Russia had a temporary military advantage over NATO in hypersonic weapons and his underestimation of Ukrainian resistance certainly contributed to the decision to start the war. One of the crucial factors was Putin's reaction to the processes in Ukrainian domestic politics and his growing conviction that Russia wouldn't be able to influence them – that Ukraine was irreversibly turning into what he called 'anti-Russia' and that there were no political means left to prevent this transformation.

One of the triggers that has been underestimated is Zelenskyi's imposition of serious sanctions on the opposition, with Viktor Medvedchuk – one of the leaders of the Opposition Platform party – a principal target.

Medvedchuk is an old hand in Ukrainian politics; formerly Kuchma's chief of staff, a personal friend of Putin and a lead negotiator in the Donbass prisoner exchanges. He is typically seen as the most 'pro-Russian' person among the major political figures in Ukraine, although one must take into account post-Euromaidan polarization and the shift of political coordinates in Ukraine to the pro-Western and nationalist pole. He was one of the targets of US sanctions after 2014. Since the Opposition Platform was ahead of Zelenskyi in the polls, it looked as though the president had just attacked a political rival. The decision to start imposing sanctions – sometimes without any serious evidence against the people they were targeting – was taken by a small group, the National Security and Defense Council (NSDC), which is basically about twenty people: mostly ministers, the heads of intelligence, counter-intelligence, the financial institutions like the central bank. One of them, Dmytro Razumkov, ex-speaker of the Ukrainian parliament, started to speak out about what was happening after he was voted out of office in October 2021, shortly before the US media first started to publish leaks about the imminent Russian invasion.

What did the sanctions against Medvedchuk and the others involve?
These sanctions were more restrictive than the ones the US usually imposes. A crucial difference is that Ukraine imposed sanctions on Ukrainian citizens without a court ruling. All Medvedchuk's bank accounts were frozen and he could not use his assets. The NSDC also sanctioned Medvedchuk's business partner Taras Kozak, the formal owner of three TV stations generally regarded as Medvedchuk's; that created a legal mechanism to stop those TV stations broadcasting, which was perhaps the most important political consequence of the sanctions – they had been strongly attacking Zelenskyi, as well as pro-Western and nationalist forces in Ukraine, typically criticizing NGO people and politicians as 'raised by Soros'. Later Zelenskyi had Medvedchuk put under house arrest, when the government started a

criminal case against him on charges of state treason for trading coal with the Donbass republics, a deal that Medvedchuk had in fact brokered for Poroshenko, because they needed coal for Ukraine's economy. In this way, Zelenskyi was able to connect Medvedchuk and Poroshenko, who were on opposite sides of Ukrainian politics; so if you connect them, they start to discredit each other; and if Poroshenko was dealing secretly with Medvedchuk, it would look like betrayal, if not treason, to an important section of his voters.

What were Zelenskyi's motives in sanctioning Medvedchuk?
It is hard to be sure about this. National-liberal civil society welcomed sanctions against Medvedchuk, whom they saw as a 'pro-Russian fifth column' – this was a move for which they waited for many years. A more realistic explanation is that Zelenskyi targeted the leader of a rival party, which was rapidly gaining popularity at the end of 2020 on the back of a wave of disenchantment with Zelenskyi among voters in the southeastern regions, who had massively supported him in 2019 but no longer saw any substantial difference between him and Poroshenko. Another aspect, which Simon Shuster underlined in his *Time* magazine story, is that the sanctions were applied, and welcomed in striking terms by the US Embassy, shortly after Biden's inauguration in late January 2021.[8]

A complicating factor is that Medvedchuk's TV stations were pushing the conspiracy theory about Hunter Biden and Burisma, which had been instrumentalized by Trump to discredit Biden during the 2020 elections. The whole world could read the transcript of the famous phone call, during which Zelenskyi did not exactly reject Trump's quid pro quo hints about starting an official Ukrainian investigation into the Burisma story, thereby throwing fuel on the fire of a scandal about Biden. Conceivably, Zelenskyi could have thought that blocking Medvedchuk's TV stations would be seen as a 'friendly gesture' towards the new US president, an attempt to whitewash himself. We also know that Biden was in no rush to give an official call to Zelenskyi after his inauguration – the fact was widely discussed in Ukrainian press at the time as a sign of possible trouble for Zelenskyi. However, we simply don't have any solid evidence to corroborate either explanation.

Whatever its motives, the Zelenskyi government then doubled down on the attack and started using sanctions much more widely – sometimes against oligarchs, often against people suspected of organized crime, but also against other opposition media. By the start of 2022, they had blocked most of the main opposition media, including one of Ukraine's most popular websites, Strana.ua, and the most popular political blogger, Anatoly Shariy, who sought asylum in the EU. Zelenskyi was creating a lot of enemies for himself with these erratic sanctions, which were legally quite dubious, and the Ukrainian oligarchs began to get worried. By the end of 2021, Zelenskyi was in conflict with Rinat Akhmetov, the richest man in Ukraine. Akhmetov started to gather popular influencers around him – well-known journalists, the dismissed speaker of the parliament Razumkov, the powerful dismissed minister of interior Avakov – and it looked like the beginning of a possible coalition against Zelenskyi that would be able to challenge him in case of some crisis, force snap elections and come to power. Zelenskyi was in a fight with the 'pro-Russian' opposition, with Poroshenko – whom he tried but failed to detain in January 2022 – and with Akhmetov. It didn't look good for him at all; if you create so many enemies, they might unite just to get rid of you. There were discussions about weakening the powers of the president, turning the position into a largely ceremonial role, moving towards a parliamentary republic. Before the war, the polls were not good for him, and in some he was even losing to Poroshenko. But the war changed everything – and, of course, Zelenskyi is now much more popular than he was. If he's able to win the war, or at least to reach some non-humiliating settlement with Putin, he may turn out to be one of the most popular political leaders that Ukraine has ever had.

How did these sanctions against Medvedchuk and others connect to the invasion?

As Shuster spelt out in his *Time* article, the sanctions against Medvedchuk in late January 2021 were followed just a few weeks later by the first signs of Russia's build-up on the Ukrainian border. Putin was able to take the exclusion of Medvedchuk from Ukrainian politics as a clear message — 'an absolutely obvious purge of the political field', Shuster's informant quotes him as saying. The US Embassy in Kiev underlined it by endorsing the sanctions immediately: the NSDC took the decision on a Friday evening, and on Saturday the US Embassy tweeted something like, 'We support Ukraine's efforts to protect its sovereignty and territorial integrity through sanctions.' We could perhaps speculate that the move against Medvedchuk was seen by Putin as the last straw; that Ukraine would never, ever implement the Minsk Accords; that no Russia-friendly politician would ever be allowed into the governmental coalition in Ukraine; that it would never be amenable to Russian interests.

The Time magazine story describes Moscow's rationale for the troop build-up, as a form of coercive diplomacy — the only way to get the West to negotiate over sanctions and security guarantees, according to Shuster's anonymous Kremlin source. It doesn't explain the invasion — or, of course, justify it.

Of course there cannot be any acceptable justification for this war, let alone from a progressive point of view. The war aimed to assert Russia's Great Power status, to mark the boundaries of its 'sphere of influence' where Russia would be in the right — able to proceed either with changing the 'anti-Russian' regime, or with the partition of Ukraine, or with turning a large territory into a huge grey zone bombed into a pre-modern state. An act inevitably leading to mass casualties, massacres of civilians, disastrous destruction. The war also serves as an important domestic goal for Putin. It aims to transform Russia's politics from post-Soviet Caesarism, whose fragility has become so evident during the recent uprisings in Belarus and

Kazakhstan, to a potentially more stable, consolidated, mobilizationist political regime with an imperialist-conservative ideological project, more hegemonic for some but more repressive for others. In this project, many Ukrainians would need to be forcibly 're-educated' to move from a 'Banderovite' anti-Russian Ukrainian identity to a *maloros* pro-Russian Ukrainian identity.

Whatever the problems post-Euromaidan Ukraine had – and there were many: messy incompetent politics, cynical, predatory oligarchy, deepening dependency on the Western powers, neoliberal reforms instead of progressive change, nationalist-radicalization trends, narrowing space for political pluralism, intensifying repression of the opposition – these were all Ukrainian problems that Ukrainians should and could solve themselves in a political process, without Russian tanks and bombs. Virtually no major Ukrainian politician or opinion leader welcomed the invasion, even those who had been labelled 'pro-Russian' for many years.

Last year, in response to questions from Russians on what Russia could do to help 'pro-Russian' people in Ukraine, a Ukrainian 'pro-Russian' opposition journalist posted something like this: 'Leave Ukraine alone and focus on building an affluent and attractive Russia.' The answer reflects a fundamental post-Soviet crisis of hegemony: the incapacity of the post-Soviet and specifically Russian ruling class to lead, not simply rule over, subaltern classes and nations. Putin, like other post-Soviet Caesarist leaders, has ruled through a combination of repression, balance and passive consent legitimated by a narrative of restoring stability after the post-Soviet collapse in the 1990s. But he has not offered any attractive developmental project. Russia's invasion should be analyzed precisely in this context: lacking sufficient soft power of attraction, the Russian ruling clique has ultimately decided to rely on the hard power of violence, starting from coercive diplomacy in the beginning of 2021, then abandoning diplomacy for military coercion in 2022.

In the build-up to the invasion, from December 2021, the Biden Administration was refusing to negotiate with Putin and instead publicizing its intelligence about Russian invasion plans and conducting megaphone diplomacy. How was that seen in Ukraine?

Until 24 February, most Ukrainians didn't believe Russia would invade. The government didn't believe it. Zelenskyi thought there might be some 'limited invasion', but not the full-scale onslaught which actually took place. Ukrainian military analysts from a Ministry of Defence think-tank produced a report saying it was extremely unlikely that Putin would attack Ukraine in 2022. Zelenskyi was unhappy with the Western media campaign, thinking it was intended to put pressure on him to start implementing the Minsk Accords, which he resisted; or perhaps to abandon the claim to join NATO. It turned out they were wrong, and the CIA and MI6 were right – although they have now informed the media that the signs of Putin's final decision to start the war appeared no earlier than February.[9] At the same time, the US and UK grossly underestimated the potential of the Ukrainian Army, just as they overestimated the Russian Army, which they expected to take Kiev in three or four days. Or, at least, they publicly projected such forecasts, which complemented apparent Russian miscalculation about a quick and easy victory for their 'special operation' in Ukraine.

So why did Washington not prevent the invasion? If they knew that an invasion was coming, why did they do nothing except leak Putin's plans to the media? One strategy would have been to start serious negotiations with Putin, to agree that Ukraine would not become a member of NATO, because they never had any desire to invite it to join – nor do they have any desire to fight for it, as we see now. Another, opposite strategy would have been to send a massive supply of weapons to Ukraine before the war started, which was sufficient to change the calculations on Putin's side. But they didn't do either of those things – and that looks sort of strange, and of course very tragic for Ukraine.

The relative strength of the Ukrainian military resistance has also surprised many observers. To what extent do you think that's due to the professional weapons and training that came from the US, and to what extent to the spirit of spontaneous national self-defence?

The military resistance is definitely stronger than the Russians expected. Besides in the occupied cities, there have been significant rallies in support of Ukraine, although so far these have involved only a small minority of residents. For example, in Kherson, a city of three hundred thousand residents before the invasion, the rallies mobilized around two to three thousand people. Some people are scared of Russian repression but some are waiting to see what will happen, how long the Russians are going to stay. Since Russian plans for the occupied territories outside of Donbass are unclear, it would be very risky to start collaborating, because when the Ukrainians come back, those people will be persecuted. This influences the calculation about collaborationism. Resistance is significant, but it is not the only thing that is happening; different Ukrainians react to the invasion in very different ways, as is typical during wars, perhaps.

In the occupied cities, are the Ukrainian political administrations still in place?

The Russians are now starting to force them to collaborate or else they are replacing them. There are reports that sometimes they arrest and kidnap Ukrainian authorities who refuse. After a month of occupation, they are starting to create some of the structures of civic military administration. They are introducing the Russian rouble as the currency in Kherson and other occupied cities in the south. They've started to pay small amounts to pensioners and public-sector employees.

Would the Zelenskyi government, or any Ukrainian government, accept the secession of the Donbass provinces or Crimea?

That would be a very painful compromise. If the government starts to say that it's ready to accept the annexation of Crimea, and the so-called independence of the Donetsk and Lugansk republics, there would be a huge attack on Zelenskyi – he is betraying the country, he has capitulated to the Russians. He would rather not say this openly, whatever is going on at the negotiating table. In a recent interview in *The Economist*, Zelenskyi said, interestingly, that it's more important to save Ukrainian lives than to save territory. That could be interpreted as thinking that he may be forced to go for this compromise. But they may calculate based on some different development in the war – the exhaustion of Russian resources, some major defeat or further US weapons supplies. They may be discussing various options which could be activated depending on the outcome on the battlefields.

What sort of Ukraine do you see emerging from this war?
The war is changing Ukrainian–Russian relations and Ukrainian identity. Before the war, a significant minority, perhaps 15 per cent, of Ukrainian citizens could say they felt themselves to be both Ukrainian and Russian. Now that will be much more difficult – they would be making a choice and, I think, one in favour of Ukrainian identity. The position of the Russian language and Russian culture will be even more restricted in the public sphere – and in private communication. In the case of a prolonged war that would turn Ukraine into a Syria or Afghanistan in Europe, there would be a strong likelihood that radical nationalists would begin to occupy leading positions in the resistance, with obvious political consequences. The Ukraine in which I was born, and where I lived most of my life, is lost now, forever – however this war ends.

Do you foresee any political ricochet effects against Putin in Russia?
Not right now. Support for the war in Russia is reported to be 60–70 per cent or more. There is a separate discussion about the extent to which we can believe Russian polls, but we don't have any other systematic evidence, and it's plausible. Of course, if the casualties grow higher, if the war drags on and the full effects of the sanctions are felt more by ordinary Russians,

perceptions will change – the Russian government would need to adapt. Just relying on dictatorial measures cannot work in the long run, and at some point they will need to start buying the loyalty of Russians. Their first problem is how to reorient the Russian economy away from the West. But right now, revolt is very unlikely, especially since about two hundred thousand of the true opposition and anti-war Russians have fled the country. The opposition in Russia is split and repressed – the Navalny movement has been crushed for now, and the Communist Party is actually backing the war. An elite coup d'état against Putin is more likely, but I doubt they would make the first move before a defeat in Ukraine. And so, in the end, it's not a revolution or a palace coup that will end the war in Ukraine, but rather the outcomes of the war that will determine whether Russia sees a revolt, a coup or the consolidation of Putinism.

Notes

Preface: A Wrong Ukrainian

1   Adam Tooze, 'Welcome to the world of the polycrisis', *Financial Times*, 28 October 2022.

2   The recently published books written in this tradition that review these discussions between Bolshevik leaders and 'Ukrainian Marxists' are Stephen Velychenko, *Painting Imperialism and Nationalism Red: The Ukrainian Marxist Critique of Russian Communist Rule in Ukraine, 1918–1925*, Toronto 2015; and Marko Bojcun, *The Workers' Movement and the National Question in Ukraine, 1897–1918*, Leiden 2021.

3   For example, Volodymyr Ishchenko, 'Left divergence, right convergence: anarchists, Marxists, and nationalist polarization in the Ukrainian conflict, 2013–14', *Globalizations*, vol. 17, no. 5, 2020, pp. 820–39, and 'Contradictions of post-Soviet Ukraine and failure of Ukraine's new left', *LeftEast*, 9 January 2020.

4   See Volodymyr Ishchenko, 'Class or regional cleavage? The Russian invasion and Ukraine's "East/West" divide', European Societies, forthcoming, for an elaboration of this argument.

5   'Konsolidatsiia ukrainskoho suspilstva: shliakhy, vyklyky, perspektyvy' [Consolidation of Ukrainian society: Paths, challenges, prospects], Razumkov Centre, 2016, p. 71.

6   S. Rudenko, 'Spetsoperatsiia "Derusyfikatsiia." Interviu z holovnym redaktorom "Istorychnoi pravdy" Vakhtanhom Kipiani' [Special operation 'Derussification': Interview with the editor-in-chief of 'Istorychna pravda' Vakhtang Kipiani], *Ukrainska Pravda*, 25 April 2022.

Recap of Events

1   For example, Lucan A. Way, *Pluralism by Default: Weak Autocrats and the Rise of Competitive Politics*, Baltimore 2015.

2   A. Kravchuk et al., 'The expected impact of the EU–Ukraine Association Agreement', Transnational Institute, 31 March 2016.

1. Ukraine Protests Are No Longer Just about Europe

1   [The attempt at a student strike quickly fizzled out. Later, I analyzed how the weakness of workers' organizations and strikes contributed to the violent radicalization of the Euromaidan, with disastrous consequences for the country. See Volodymyr Ishchenko, 'Insufficiently diverse: The problem of nonviolent leverage and radicalization of Ukraine's Maidan uprising, 2013–2014', *Journal of Eurasian Studies*, vol. 11, no. 2, 2020, pp. 201–15.]

2   [Now I would put it slightly differently. Instead of saying that Euromaidan was neither a revolution nor a coup, I would say that it combined elements of both. Revolutions and coups are not mutually exclusive. Moreover, the characteristics of revolutions like Euromaidan make them structurally predisposed to being hijacked, including for coups, by forces that do not represent the majority of participants (see Chapter 5).]

3   [See Volodymyr Ishchenko, 'Denial of the obvious: Far right in Maidan protests and their danger today', *Vox Ukraine*, 16 April 2018.]

4   [The government delayed the final verdict in the Ukrainian court system on the Communist Party's appeal, so as not to allow the party to appeal to the ECHR. After the Russian invasion, the government banned communists together with over a dozen parties labelled as 'pro-Russian'. See Chapter 6, below.]

5   [After the Russian invasion, this materialized most prominently for the Western public as the 'Ukrainian left' phenomenon, even though this small milieu has failed so far to even build a strong organization, let alone a new party: see Volodymyr Ishchenko, 'Contradictions of post-Soviet Ukraine and failure of Ukraine's new left', *LeftEast*, 9 January 2020, and also the Preface to this collection.]

2. Maidan Mythologies

1   [My analysis of this problem has evolved since 2014–15, as will become clear in Chapter 5. It is precisely the characteristics that Maidan shared with the

global wave of protests of the 2010s – poorly articulated demands, beyond 'Down with Yanukovych!'; loose organization; weak and dispersed leadership – that allowed it to be so easily hijacked by right-wing forces.]

2 [Later published in Volodymyr Ishchenko, 'Far right participation in the Ukrainian Maidan protests: An attempt of systematic estimation', *European Politics and Society*, vol. 17, no. 4, 2016, pp. 453–72.]

3 [More on this in a later article: Volodymyr Ishchenko, 'Insufficiently diverse: The problem of nonviolent leverage and radicalization of Ukraine's Maidan uprising, 2013–14', *Journal of Eurasian Studies*, vol. 11, no. 2, 2020, pp. 201–15.]

4 [See, however, my development of the class-conflict argument for the elite classes – political capitalists, professional middle class and transnational capital – in Chapter 8, below.]

3. A Comedian in a Drama

1 [Ironically, speculation about Kolomoiskyi's significant influence on Zelenskyi appears to have been proven wrong. Andrii Bohdan, a lawyer whom many perceived as a link between the two, served as Zelenskyi's chief of staff for less than a year. A small group of deputies loyal to Kolomoiskyi entered the Ukrainian parliament on Zelenskyi's party list, but even more entered outside it. Kolomoiskyi received no compensation for PrivatBank. In fact, Kolomoiskyi could be very unhappy with developments under Zelenskyi. Before the invasion, his pundits criticized the 'external management' of Ukraine by the West and 'anti-corruption' civil society. After the invasion began, he broke ranks with the Ukrainian elite and did not publicly condemn the invasion for a long time. Some of Kolomoiskyi's key property became a primary target of selective nationalizations in 2022 under military pretext.]

2 [The following may sound naive in today's post-invasion reality. However, these trends had actually begun to materialize. Zelenskyi's attacks on the political opposition and the 'oligarchs' tended to unite the most powerful elite fractions in Ukrainian politics against him, rather than consolidating his power. Neoliberal-nationalist civil society was increasingly delegitimized as a promoter of Western interests. Some new parties appeared, trying to mobilize Zelenskyi's 'betrayed majority'. But all these developments, which benefited the left in the long run, were aborted by the Russian invasion.]

4. From Ukraine with Comparisons

1   Olga Onuch and Gwendolyn Sasse, 'Anti-regime action and geopolitical polarization: Understanding protester dispositions in Belarus', *Post-Soviet Affairs*, vol. 38, nos 1–2, 2022, pp. 62–87.

2   Volodymyr Ishchenko, 'Insufficiently diverse: The problem of nonviolent leverage and radicalization of Ukraine's Maidan uprising, 2013–2014', *Journal of Eurasian Studies*, vol. 11, no. 2, 2020, pp. 201–15.

5. The Vicious Post-Soviet Circle

1   [This chapter is based on a paper co-authored with Oleg Zhuravlev, 'The Post-Soviet vicious circle: Revolution as reproduction of the crisis of hegemony', in Dylan Riley and Marco Santoro, eds, *The Anthem Companion to Gramsci*, forthcoming. It is mostly compiled from Volodymyr Ishchenko and Oleg Zhuravlev, 'How *maidan* revolutions reproduce and intensify the post-Soviet crisis of political representation', *PONARS Eurasia Policy Memo* 714, 18 October 2021; and Volodymyr Ishchenko, 'Ukraine in the vicious circle of post-Soviet crisis of hegemony', *LeftEast*, 29 October 2021.]

2   Antonio Gramsci, *Prison Notebooks: Volume 2*, New York 1996, pp. 32–3.

3   Jochen Hellbeck, *Revolution on My Mind: Writing a Diary under Stalin*, Cambridge, MA, 2009; Stephen Kotkin, *Magnetic Mountain: Stalinism as a Civilization*, Berkeley 1995; Anatoly Pinsky, 'Subjectivity after Stalin', *Russian Studies in History*, vol. 58, nos 2–3, pp. 79–88.

4   Juliane Fürst, 'Prisoners of the Soviet self? Political youth opposition in Late Stalinism', *Europe-Asia Studies*, vol. 54, no. 3, 2002, pp. 353–75.

5   For example, Pınar Bedirhanoğlu, 'The nomenklatura's passive revolution in Russia in the neoliberal era', in Leo McCann, ed., *Russian Transformations*, London 2004, pp. 19–41; Rick Simon, 'Passive revolution, perestroika and the emergence of the new Russia', *Capital & Class*, vol. 34, no. 3, 2010, pp. 429–48; Kees Van Der Pijl, 'Soviet socialism and passive revolution', in Stephen Gill, ed., *Gramsci, Historical Materialism and International Relations*, Cambridge 2011, pp. 237–58; Owen Worth, *Hegemony, International Political Economy and Post-Communist Russia*, London 2017.

6   Adam Morton, 'The continuum of passive revolution', *Capital & Class*, vol. 34, no. 3, pp. 315–42, at p. 333. See also Alex Callinicos, 'The limits of passive revolution', *Capital & Class*, vol. 34, no. 3, 2010, pp. 491–507.

7   Michael Burawoy, 'The state and economic involution: Russia through a China lens', *World Development*, vol. 24, no. 6, 1996, pp. 1105–17; Steven L.

Solnick, *Stealing the State: Control and Collapse in Soviet Institutions*, Cambridge, MA, 1998; Yakov Rabkin, 'Undoing years of progress', in Yakov Rabkin and Mikhail Minakov, eds, *Demodernization: A Future in the Past*, Stuttgart 2018, pp. 24–8.

8   Pascal Perrineau, 'The crisis in political representation', in Pascal Perrineau and Luc Rouban, eds, *Politics in France and Europe*, New York 2010, pp. 3–14.

9   Oleg Zhuravlev and Volodymyr Ishchenko, 'Exclusiveness of civic nationalism: Euromaidan eventful nationalism in Ukraine', *Post-Soviet Affairs*, vol. 36, no. 3, 2020, pp. 226–45.

10   Maxim Gatskov and Kseniia Gatskova, 'Civil society in Ukraine', in Alberto Veira-Ramos et al., eds, *Ukraine in Transformation: From Soviet Republic to European Society*, Cham 2019, pp. 123–44.

11   Mikhail Minakov, 'Republic of clans: The evolution of the Ukrainian political system', in Bálint Magyar, ed., *Stubborn Structures: Reconceptualizing Post-Communist Regimes*, Budapest 2019, pp. 217–46, at p. 240.

12   Paul Chaisty and Stephen Whitefield, 'How challenger parties can win big with frozen cleavages: Explaining the landslide victory of the Servant of the People Party in the 2019 Ukrainian parliamentary elections', *Party Politics*, vol. 28, no. 1, January 2022, pp. 115–26.

13   [As discussed in Chapter 6, below, the present war in Ukraine may lead either to the elimination of a sovereign centre of capital accumulation in the post-Soviet space, and to the latter's eventual disintegration, or to fundamental political, economic and ideological changes in Russia itself. In either case, the vicious post-Soviet cycle is coming to an end.]

6. Three Scenarios for the Ukraine–Russia Crisis

1   [Should Zelenskyi's public denials of the invasion threat on the eve of the invasion be considered irresponsible in retrospect? Some Ukrainians think so now, and may question Zelenskyi and his team even more harshly after the war is over. Should I be ashamed of my feelings and of questioning the 'imminent invasion' narrative? In all the self-congratulatory reports of the US and British elites (e.g. Erin Banco et al., 'Something was badly wrong: When Washington realized Russia was actually invading Ukraine', *Politico*, 24 February 2023), I have seen no convincing explanation as to why so little was done to prevent the invasion by those who claimed its 'imminence' several months before it began – neither supplying arms to Ukraine much earlier nor negotiating seriously with Putin; there was practically nothing but an information campaign. Its aim was not to prevent the invasion, but to ensure Western consolidation against Russia after it had begun. The campaign

left most of the European and Ukrainian elites unconvinced until the very last days. As is now well documented, Ukraine was only preparing for a limited Russian offensive in Donbass and 'hybrid' destabilization (Mykhaylo Zabrodskyi et al., 'Preliminary lessons in conventional warfighting from Russia's invasion of Ukraine: February–July 2022', Royal United Services Institute, 30 November 2022, pp. 22–3). I wrote this op-ed in early February 2022, outlining what the Ukrainian government could and should do to preserve the chance for a pluralistic and sovereign Ukraine – a chance to get my country back that was cut short by the Russian invasion.]

2   Samuel Charap, 'How to break the cycle of conflict with Russia', *Foreign Affairs*, 7 February 2022.

3   Samuel Charap et al., eds, *A Consensus Proposal for a Revised Regional Order in Post-Soviet Europe and Eurasia*, Rand Corporation, 2019.

4   'Zahroza novoho vtorhnennya: hromads′ka dumka pro konflikt, mozhlyvi kompromisy ta protydiyu Rosiyi' [The threat of a new invasion: Public opinion on the conflict, possible compromises and counteracting Russia], Ilko Kucheriv Foundation, 2 February 2022.

5   'Yesli Zapadu budet vygodno – prodast Ukrainu' [If it is profitable for the West, it will sell Ukraine], Gazeta.ua, 24 September 2019.

6   [See Volodymyr Ishchenko, 'The Minsk Accords and the Political Weaknes of the "Other Ukraine"', *Russian Politics*, vol. 8, no. 2, 2023, pp. 127–46, for a detailed analysis of the domestic contention in Ukraine over the Minsk Accords and the fundamental problem of the inability of the 'Eastern' camp in Ukrainian politics to articulate a positive program for Ukraine's pluralist national development and to support it with sustained civic mobilization.]

7   Adam Tooze, 'What if Putin's war regime turns to MMT [Modern Monetary Theory]?', *Chartbook*, 3 March 2022.

8   Anastasiya Tovt, ' "Sanktsii stali biznesom": Kak vnosyatsya oshibki i "ispravleniya" v sanktsionnyye spiski SNBO' ['"Sanctions have become business": How "errors" and "corrections" are made to the NSDC sanctions lists'], Strana.ua, 23 November 2021.

9   [Indeed, in the course of 2022, they changed the law and permanently banned these parties and more under an expedited procedure. In addition, the government pressured a number of opposition MPs to resign and turned the remaining 'pro-Russian' deputies into even more loyal supporters of Zelenskyi than the 'pro-Western' parties: Igor Burdyga, 'These are the men Russia wanted to put in charge of Ukraine', *openDemocracy*, 4 March 2023.]

10   [According to one estimate, there were indeed relatively more collaborators with the Russians from the banned parties. However, the absolute majority of elected officials and members of local councils from these parties remained loyal to Ukraine, which raises even more questions about the reasons and

motives for their ban and stigmatization as 'pro-Russian': Kateryna Bereziuk, 'U yakykh partiiakh zradnykiv naibilshe?', [Which parties have more traitors?], *Chesno*, 17 March 2023.]

11 Sergey Faldin, 'Is Russia's silent majority waking up?', *Al Jazeera*, 20 October 2022.

12 Adam Tooze, 'Warfare without the state: New Keynesian shock therapy for Ukraine's home front', *Chartbook*, 22 October 2022.

7. NATO through Ukrainian Eyes

1 Natalia Panina, ed., *Ukrainske suspilstvo 1994–2004: stsiolohichnyi monitorynh* [Ukrainian Society 1994–2004: Sociological Monitoring], Kiev 2004, p. 16; 'Stavlennia hromadian do intehratsiinykh proektiv' [The Attitude of Citizens to Integration Projects], Kiev International Institute of Sociology (KIIS), 20 March 2012. All KIIS polls cited in this chapter are available at kiis.com.ua.

2 For example, F. Stephen Larrabee, 'Ukraine at the crossroads', *Washington Quarterly*, vol. 30, no. 4, September 2007, pp. 45–61, at p. 49.

3 Studies show no correlation between support for NATO membership and perceived level of knowledge about the organization. See Valerii Khmelko, 'Stavlennia hromadian Ukrainy do yii vstupu do Yevrosoiuzu i NATO ta yikhni otsinky svoyei obiznanosti stosovno tsykh orhanizatsii' [Attitudes of Ukrainian citizens towards joining the EU and NATO and their assessment of their knowledge about these organizations], *Sotsiolohiia: teoriia, metody, marketynh*, no. 1, 2006, pp. 71–87.

4 Panina, *Ukrainske suspilstvo 1994–2004: sotsiolohichnyi monitorynh*, p. 16; Andrii Bychenko, 'Hromadska dumka pro NATO i pryiednannia do nioho Ukrainy' [Public Opinion on NATO and Ukraine's NATO Membership], *Natsionalna bezpeka i oborona*, 2006, p. 21.

5 Bychenko, 'Hromadska dumka pro NATO i pryiednannia do nioho Ukrainy', p. 36; Khmelko, 'Stavlennia hromadian Ukrainy do yii vstupu do Yevrosoiuzu i NATO ta yikhni otsinky svoyei obiznanosti stosovno tsykh orhanizatsii'. Although the alliance enjoyed somewhat higher approval in the western regions than in the east, no pro-NATO majority existed in the former prior to 2014.

6 Political capitalists, in the sense I employ the term here, represent the fraction of the capitalist class whose main competitive advantage derives from selective benefits bestowed by the state, unlike capitalists who look to exploit technological innovations or a particularly cheap labour force. See Chapter 8, below.

7 Oleksii V. Haran and Mariia Zolkina, 'The demise of Ukraine's "Eurasian vector" and the rise of pro-NATO sentiment', *PONARS Eurasia Policy Memo* 458, 16 February 2017.

8   Stephen F. Cohen, *Soviet Fates and Lost Alternatives: From Stalinism to the New Cold War*, New York 2011, p. 191.

9   Serhii Leshchenko, 'Yuliia Tymoshenko: het vid Aliansu!' [Yulia Tymoshenko: Away from the Alliance!], *Ukrainska pravda*, 11 February 2009.

10 Igor Guzhva, Olesia Medvedeva and Maksim Minin, 'Na grani voiny. Timoshenko snova premier, gibel 106 shakhterov. Chem zhila strana v 2007 godu' [On the Brink of War. Tymoshenko is prime minister again, the Death of 106 Miners. What the Country Experienced in 2007], *Strana News*, 11 August 2021.

11 Dominique Arel, 'Ukraine since the War in Georgia', *Survival*, vol. 50, no. 6, December 2008, pp. 15–25, at pp. 18–19.

12 Haran and Zolkina, 'The demise of Ukraine's "Eurasian vector" and the rise of Pro-NATO sentiment'.

13 Ibid.

14 There were no doubt technical and methodological hurdles to polling in these areas. However, nationalist outcry over the 'treasonous' findings of the periodic surveys that were carried out in Crimea and the parts of Donbass not controlled by the Ukrainian government raises the question of whether *political* considerations were no less decisive in the choice to omit the opinions of a significant part of the population (never officially deducted from national tallies). See Andrii Gladun, 'Sotsiolohiia ta ideolohiia: dyskusiia shchodo opytuvan pro nastroi krymchan' [Sociology and ideology: A discussion regarding surveys of the attitudes of Crimeans], *Commons: Journal of Social Criticism*, 28 April 2015; Gwendolyn Sasse, 'The Donbas – Two parts, or still one? The experience of war through the eyes of the regional population', *ZOiS*, 2 May 2017. This is all the more peculiar in light of the regular polling conducted in parts of southeastern Ukraine of population dislocations and a moving front line, occupied by Russia in 2022, despite even more serious concerns about reliability as a result of population dislocations and a moving front line.

15 Gerard Toal, John O'Loughlin and Kristin M. Bakke, 'Is Ukraine caught between Europe and Russia? We asked Ukrainians this important question', *Washington Post*, 26 February 2020; 'Suspilno-politychni oriientatsii naselennia Ukrainy' [Socio-political orientations of the population of Ukraine], KIIS, April 2020.

16 'Dumky ta pohliady naselennia Ukrainy: lypen 2020' [The opinions and views of the population of Ukraine: July 2020], Social Monitoring Center, 21 July 2020.

17 'Suspilna pidtrymka yevroatlantychnoho kursu Ukrainy: otsinky ta rekomendatsii' [The public support for Ukraine's Euro-Atlantic course: Assessment and recommendations], Razumkov Centre, 2021; available at razumkov.org.ua.

18   'Ukraine is the only non-NATO country supporting every NATO mission', the president declaimed ahead of the Bucharest Summit. Steven Lee Myers, 'Bush backs Ukraine's bid to join NATO', *New York Times*, 1 April 2008.

19   'Heopolitychni oriientatsii zhytelliv Ukrainy: cherven 2021 roku' [Geopolitical orientations of the residents of Ukraine: June 2021], KIIS, 18 July 2021; Olga Onuch and Javier Perez Sandoval, 'A majority of Ukrainians support joining NATO. Does this matter?', *Washington Post*, 4 February 2022.

20   For example, Alexander J. Motyl, 'Ukraine's TV president is dangerously pro-Russian', *Foreign Policy*, 1 April 2019.

21   Serhii Kudelia, 'NATO or bust: Why do Ukraine's leaders dismiss neutrality as a security Strategy?', *Russia Matters*, 9 February 2022.

22   Volodymyr Ishchenko and Małgorzata Kulbaczewska-Figat, 'Why Russia's political capitalists went to war – And how the war could end their rule', *Cross-Border Talks*, 29 July 2022.

23   Especially after the repression and marginalization of the left parties that did have some ability to mobilize their supporters. See Volodymyr Ishchenko, 'The Ukrainian left during and after the Maidan protests', Study for the Left in the European Parliament, January 2016.

24   'Civic space and fundamental freedoms in Ukraine, 1 November 2019–31 October 2021', United Nations Human Rights, Office of the High Commissioner, Ukraine 2021.

25   In the wording of the survey, the two options were not mutually exclusive. 'Mozhlyvosti ta oereshkody na shliakhu demokratychnoho perekhodu Ukrainy' [Opportunities and obstacles on the way of Ukraine's democratic transition], KIIS, 2–11 May 2022.

26   'Opytuvannia NDI: mozhlyvosti ta oereshkody na shliakhu demokratych-noho perekhodu Ukrainy' [NDI survey: Opportunities and obstacles on the way of Ukraine's democratic transition], KIIS, 20 September 2022.

27   'Nastroi ta otsinky ukrainskykh bizhentsiv (lypen- serpen 2022 r.)' [Moods and evaluations of Ukrainian refugees (June–August 2022)], Razumkov Centre, 30 August 2022.

28   On the basis of an experiment conducted in May 2022, researchers at the KIIS estimate that the spiral of silence contributed an additional 4–6 per cent to pro-Western positions. 'Pryiniatnist vidmovy vid vstupu do NATO pry otry-manni harantii bezpeky vid okremykh krain: rezultaty telefonnoho opytu-vannia, provedenoho 13–18 travnia 2022 roku' [The acceptability of Ukraine's refusal to join NATO on conditions of security guarantees from certain countries: Results of a telephone survey on 13–18 May 2022], KIIS, 24 May 2022.

29   The Gradus poll had its limitations: it was restricted to city dwellers with access to smartphones, and slightly skewed to the more urbanized southeast of

the country; however, it did not include people over the age of sixty, who are generally less supportive of NATO. 'The attitudes, emotions, and actions of Ukrainians during the full-scale war between Russia and Ukraine', Gradus, April 2022; available at gradus.app.

30 'Pryiniatnist vidmovy vid vstupu do NATO', KIIS, 24 May 2022.

31 'Results – 2022: Under the Blue-Yellow Flag of Freedom!' Democratic Initiatives Foundation, 5 January 2023; available at dif.org.

32 WSJ/NORC Ukraine Poll June 2022; available at norc.org.

33 'Perception index of the Russian-Ukrainian War: Results of a telephone survey conducted on 19–24 May 2022', KIIS, 27 May 2022.

34 'Hromadska dumka v Ukraini pislia 10 misiatsiv viiny' [Public opinion in Ukraine after 10 months of war], KIIS, 15 January 2023.

8. Behind Russia's War Is Thirty Years of Post-Soviet Class Conflict

1 Steven L. Solnick, *Stealing the State: Control and Collapse in Soviet Institutions*, Cambridge, MA 1998.

2 Ruslan Dzarasov, 'Insider rent makes Russian capitalism: A rejoinder to Simon Pirani', *Journal of Contemporary Central and Eastern Europe*, vol. 19, no. 3, 2011, pp. 585–97.

3 Iván Szelényi, 'Capitalisms after communism', *New Left Review* 96, Nov–Dec 2015.

4 Göran Therborn, *What Does the Ruling Class Do When It Rules?* London, 1978.

5 Branko Milanović, 'Can corruption be good for growth?', *Brave New Europe*, 29 June 2020.

6 'Mark Beissinger on contemporary urban civic revolutions', *Democracy Paradox* [podcast], 12 April 2022.

7 Branko Milanović, 'Russia's war shows the chaos in the world order', *Jacobin*, 21 March 2022.

9. Ukrainian Voices?

1 As Mark Beissinger has established on the basis of a mass of quantitative data; see *The Revolutionary City: Urbanization and the Global Transformation of Rebellion*, Princeton 2022. For 'deficient revolutions', see Volodymyr Ishchenko and Oleg Zhuravlev, 'How Maidan revolutions reproduce and intensify the post-Soviet crisis of political representation', *PONARS Eurasia Policy Memo No. 714*, 18 October 2021, and Chapter 5 in this book.

2   Anna Jikhareva and Kaspar Surber, 'Ukraine shouldn't become a neoliberal laboratory', *Jacobin*, 17 September 2022; Peter Korotaev, 'Ukraine's war economy is being choked by neoliberal dogmas', *Jacobin*, 14 July 2022; Luke Cooper, 'Market economics in an all-out-war?', LSE Research Report, 1 December 2022.

3   Aris Roussinos, 'Did Ukraine need a war?', *UnHerd*, 1 July 2022.

4   Cooper, 'Market economics in an all-out-war?'

5   Chi Chi Shi, 'Defining my own oppression: Neoliberalism and the demand of victimhood', *Historical Materialism*, vol. 26, no. 2, 2018, pp. 271–95.

6   Nancy Fraser, 'From redistribution to recognition? Dilemmas of justice in a "post-socialist" age', *New Left Review* 212, July–August 1995, pp. 68–93.

7   Iryna Podolyak, 'Why Russians are to blame for Putin', *Visegrad/Insight*, 16 March 2022.

8   Olesya Khromeychuk, 'Where is Ukraine?', *RSA*, 13 June 2022.

9   George Packer, 'Ukrainians are defending the values Americans claim to hold', *Atlantic*, October 2022.

10   Nataliya Gumenyuk, 'Russia's invasion is making Ukraine more democratic', *Atlantic*, 16 July 2022.

11   US National Democratic Institute, 'Opportunities and challenges facing Ukraine's democratic transition', August 2022; Iryna Balachuk, 'Majority of Ukrainians want strong leader, not democracy during war – KMIS', *Ukrainska Pravda*, 18 August 2022.

12   Anton Oleinik, 'Volunteers in Ukraine: From provision of services to state- and nation-building', *Journal of Civil Society*, 18 September 2018, pp. 364–85.

13   Alexander Maxwell, 'Popular and scholarly primordialism: The politics of Ukrainian history during Russia's 2022 invasion of Ukraine', *Journal of Nationalism, Memory and Language Politics*, vol. 16, no. 1, October 2022, pp. 152–71.

14   Mark Beissinger, 'Revolutions have succeeded more often in our time, but their consequences have become more ambiguous', CEU Democracy Institute, 8 April 2022.

Interview: Towards the Abyss

1   Volodymyr Ishchenko and Oleg Zhuravlev, 'How maidan revolutions repro- duce and intensify the post-Soviet crisis of political representation', *PONARS Eurasia Policy Memo* 714, 18 October 2021, and Chapter 5 in this book.

2   Volodymyr Ishchenko, 'Insufficiently diverse: The problem of nonviolent leverage and radicalization of Ukraine's Maidan uprising, 2013–14', *Journal of Eurasian Studies*, vol. 11, no. 2, 2020, pp. 201–15.

3   Ishchenko, 'Ukraine's fractures', *New Left Review* 87, May–June 2014.

4   Volodymyr Ishchenko, 'Nationalist radicalization trends in post-Euromaidan Ukraine', *PONARS Eurasia*, Policy Memo 529, May 2018.

5   Oleg Zhuravlev and Volodymyr Ishchenko, 'Exclusiveness of civic nationalism: Euromaidan eventful nationalism in Ukraine', *Post-Soviet Affairs*, vol. 36, no. 3, 2020, pp. 226–45.

6   [This actually backfired on Zelenskyi. He had to dismiss his loyalist chief of counter-intelligence and also the prosecutor general in July 2022 when it appeared that even some high-ranking officers in their structures collaborated with Russians. See 'Zelenskiy fires Ukraine's spy chief and top state prosecutor', *Guardian*, 17 July 2022.]

7   [According to a later and widely cited analysis by the Royal United Services Institute, the Kremlin did indeed bet on the destabilization of the Ukrainian government for the success of its 'special military operation'; however, it rushed ahead with the full-scale invasion plan before the prerequisite of a full-blown political crisis materialized: Jack Watling, Oleksandr V Danylyuk and Nick Reynolds, 'Preliminary lessons from Russia's unconventional operations during the Russo-Ukrainian War, February 2022–February 2023', RUSI, 29 March 2023.]

8   Simon Shuster, 'The untold story of the Ukraine crisis', *Time*, 2 February 2022.

9   James Risen, 'US intelligence says Putin made a last-minute decision to invade Ukraine', *Intercept*, 11 March 2022.